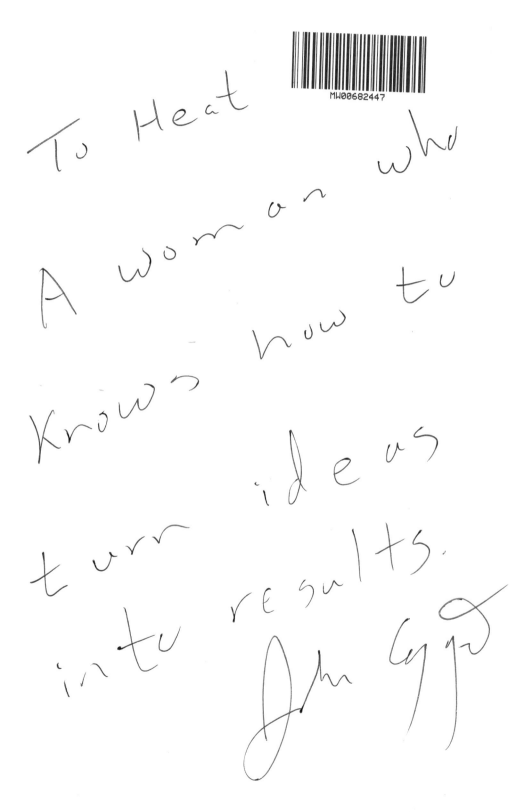

To Heat

A woman who

knows how to

turn ideas

into results.

LEADING THROUGH
IDEAS
A PRACTICAL FRAMEWORK
BY JOHN EGGERT, PH.D

Printed in the United States of America

First Printing, 2014

ISBN 978-0-9907957-0-4

The Idea Leadership Company
1822-C Southmore
Houston, Texas 77004
www.leadingthroughideas.com

TABLE OF CONTENTS

DEDICATION

This book is dedicated to
Karl and Doris Eggert, and Claude and Sue Rodgers,
who laid the path, and to

Karla, Tim, Catherine and Paul,
who took that path a bit further, and to

Forrest Nottingham as well as Derek, Owen, Audrey and Bryce,
who will follow in all of our footsteps,
taking their ideas to places we can't even imagine.

ACKNOWLEDGEMENTS

First of all, I acknowledge and thank my wife, Pamela Rodgers, for her limitless support and faith in me. She has shown unreasonable patience as she watched me plod forward on a very circuitous route. Pam's professional experience in organization effectiveness and leadership development has provided me with unique and important insights at several key junctures in the development of this book.

Many of the sixty-five members of the Executive Panel, described in detail in the following section, provided important feedback on various portions of early drafts of this book. However, four deserve special mention for laboring through entire early drafts. Their recommendations led to significant reorganizations of the content and increased clarity of the text. These are John Andresen, Greg Panagos, John Robb and Richard Walsh. I'd also like to thank my colleagues Bruce Anderson. David Daugherty, Nate Ellis, Jess Kozman, Margaret Maat and Matt Williams for their advice and moral support.

Almost all of what I have learned about making ideas happen in organizational environments has been taught to me by the hundreds of clients with whom I have partnered over the past several decades—particularly those who participated in the in-depth interviews twenty years ago that served as a foundation for this book. The examples and case studies herein have come from these generous people, although I have frequently changed key details and sometimes merged cases to ensure their anonymity. I owe all a debt of gratitude.

I thank my siblings, Paul, Carol, Laurie and, especially, Nancy—who not only comes up with wild and crazy ideas but also makes them happen—for the intellectual stimulation, role modeling, and familial support they have provided throughout my life. And, I thank my children, Karla, Tim, Catherine and Paul for their encouragement and for hardly ever asking, "Is your book done yet?"

Finally, particular thanks and praise are due to my manuscript consultant and writing coach, Tacey A. Rosolowski, Ph.D., who has a gift for unscrewing screwed up ideas. She has provided invaluable help as I endured the writing process and refined my concepts and clarity of language. I also thank Daniel Maddux of Elite Documentation Inc. for his technical proofing and Jenny Conte, of Sharp Egg, Inc., for her excellent assistance in layout and design.

I ask forgiveness of those I have neglected to mention by name, and I lay claim to whatever conceptual fuzziness or errors in fact or logic that remain.

ACKNOWLEDGEMENT OF
THE EXECUTIVE PANEL

A special acknowledgment is due to a group of loyal supporters who were kind enough to participate in interviews, complete a series of surveys, attend a seminar, review drafts, discuss ideas, and otherwise provide significant insights and moral support to my work. Most of this occurred over the past two years, but several panel members participated in extended interviews over 20 years ago. These generous people are listed below.

*Those marked with an asterisk also participated in the in-depth interviews from 1993 to 1995 that provided the initial foundation for this book.

***Tom Allin**, CEO, Jollibee Foods Corporation, Manila, Philippines. Previously: Founder & Majority Owner, Chow Fun Holdings; Managing Director, Security Capital Group; President, McDonald's Development Company Europe-McDonald's Corp.

Bruce M. Anderson, President Thinking Partners, Inc. Previously: VP Organizational Consulting, Right Management Consultants; VP Human Resources, Naylor Industries.

John Andresen SPHR GPHR, HR Consultant. Previously: Corporate Human Resources Manager, Geokinetics; Director of Human Resources, Air Liquide Engineering & Construction.

Larry Andrews, President, Depromark, LLC. Previously: SVP, ATM & in-store strategy, SunTrust bank; SVP, Texas Group Manager, Washington Mutual Bank.

Linda Berger, Chief Accounting Officer, Direct Energy. Previously: Vice President of Finance, Upstream & Trading, Direct Energy; CFO, North America Gas, Power and NGLs Trading, BP; CFO, European Natural Gas and Global LNG Trading, BP.

David Blake, President, Blake Healthcare Consultants. Previously: Vice President, National Contracting, CIGNA Healthcare; Vice President, Network and Clinical Operations, Methodist Health Services.

Al Bolea, Leadership Consultant for Oil, Gas, and Energy Industries. Previously: President BP Transportation, BP Exploration (Alaska); CEO/General Manager, Dubai Petroleum.

Sharon Brownfield, Chief Learning Officer, Seven Hills Foundation; Partner, Brownfield & Lent. Previously: Executive Director, Training and Development, American Red Cross; Director, GlaxoSmithKline (GSK).

John Burgess, Owner, Smith and Burgess.

John F Burke, Partner and COO, CPI Houston. Previously: General Manager of the LHH Houston office; Principal/partner of a Houston area Talent Development/Consulting firm in the Oil and Gas, Energy and Medical arena.

Sanjay Chadha, Vice President and Chief Information Officer, Melior Technology. Previously: CTO, Director of Strategy, Architecture and Portfolio, El Paso Corporation; Chief Information Technology Architect & PMO, LyondellBasell Industries.

*Terri Craig, Retired. Previously: Sr. Director-Operations, McDonald's Corporation; Sr. Director-Training, McDonald's Corporation; National Training Multi-Department Head, McDonald's Corporation.

David Daugherty, President, The Daugherty Group; Executive Coach/ Organizational Consultant / Speaker.

Bruce Davis, Bruce R Davis Life Science Consulting; Previously: Senior Vice President, Manufacturing, Inspiration Biopharmaceuticals, Inc; Senior Vice President, Manufacturing Development, Bluebird Biosciences, Inc.

Shari Davis, Director of Project Controls, Estimating and Execution, Audubon Engineering, LP. Previously: Director of Quality, Audubon Engineering, LP; Global Manager, Project Systems Management, Mustang Engineering, LP.

David Dezelan, President of Lakeland Healthcare Specialty. Previously: Corporate Director of Managed Care and a 36-year career in Pharmaceutical Sales and Marketing for Abbott Laboratories.

John Drengenberg, Consumer Safety Director, UL (Underwriters Laboratories LLC).

Paul Eggert, Retired. Previously: 35-year career in a federal agency, ending as a multi-state field manager.

Nate Ellis, Senior Oil & Gas Relationship Manager, International Banking. Previously: Director, Bank of Tokyo-Mitsubishi; Director, Enron; SVP, Mizuho Corporate Bank.

Sudhir Golikeri, Gas Processing Technology Manager for Bechtel Hydrocarbon Technology Solutions, Inc. Previously: Senior Research Associate, BP Amoco; Principal Process Engineer, International Process Services.

Carol Grosso, most recent role as IT Process, Reporting & Services Director at Technip. Previously: Director of IT Service Delivery at Global Industries; IT Operations Services Senior Manager, LyondellBasell Industries.

Kenneth Guidry, President, PKF Texas. Previously: Past Chairman and Member of the Board of Directors, PKF North America; Director, Chief Operating Officer and Audit Practice Leader, PKF Texas.

Joel Guillaume, Furnace Technology Manager, Technip Stone & Webster Process Technology.

John Hall, Founder and former President and CEO, Spectrum Design Services, Inc. and SDS Management Services, Inc. Currently Project Director for International Alliance Group.

Jim Hamilton, Senior Project Manager, Wipro Technologies. Previously: IT Director, TPC Group; Principal Consultant, JCHamilton Consulting; Senior IT Director, ExxonMobil.

Kyle J. Hart, PE, Director of Engineering and Construction, Gathering and Processing Division, Enbridge. Previously: Manager, Engineering and Construction, Gathering and Processing Division, Enbridge; Operations Manager, East Texas, Enbridge.

Georganne Hodges, CFO, Spark Energy. Previously: Vice President Finance, Direct Energy Residential; Vice President Finance, Direct Energy Upstream.

*Linda M. Hopkins, Retired. Previously: Managing Director & SVP with Continental Bank and Bank of America; Litigation Project Management Consultant.

John J Hopper, Chief Financial Officer, Melior Technology, Inc. Previously: Vice President and Treasurer, El Paso Corporation; Corporate Cash Manager / Principal Analyst El Paso Natural Gas Company.

Luis Yofe. Senior Business Leader, Travel Payment Solutions, MasterCard—Global Products & Solutions.

McCall Keyser, Accounting Consultant. Previously: Senior Director of Internal Control and IT, TPC Group (Formerly Texas Petrochemicals); Director of Finance/Div Controller, Coca-Cola Enterprises.

Bruce Klein, Retired. Previously: Chief Financial Officer, CLARCOR Inc.

Margaret Kneeland, Strategic Program Manager, Public Sector, Cisco Systems, Inc. Previously: Regional Sales Manager, Cisco Systems, Inc.

Jess Kozman, SouthEast Asia Regional Manager: Exploration & Production Applications - Information Management at Mubadala Petroleum. Previously: Management and consulting in Oil & Gas Operators, Service Companies, Software Business Development and Data Management.

*Dave Kreischer, Managing Partner, Higgins Kreischer & Associate. Previously: Senior Partner, Baiocchi and Associates; Vice President, Human Resources Development, Citicorp.

Timur Kuru, VP of Engineering, Manufacturing & Operations Support, Key Energy Services. Previously: VP & GM of Drilling Systems, LeTourneau Technologies; VP of Corporate Development and Treasurer, Forum Oilfield Technologies.

*Patricia Lammers, Consultant.

Chuck Laughter, Vice President - Engineering & Operations, Joule Processing. Previously: Vice President, Midstream, Audubon Engineering; Vice President, Strategic Account Management, Audubon Engineering; Vice President, Projects Business Unit and Board of Directors, Wilson-Mohr, Inc.

Jorge Lebrija, Global Sourcing Director at Ensco plc. Previously: Director, Procurement, Baker Hughes; various sourcing management roles at Transocean and CEMEX.

Margaret Maat, Organizational Change Consultant and Leadership Coach.

Brian Maddox, CEO, Trailhead Engineering, LLC. Previously: Managing Partner and CEO at Audubon Engineering; Division Manager, Berwanger, Inc.

****Lynn McPheeters**, retired VP and CFO, Caterpillar Inc.

Yogendra Mehta, Director, Global Services, Oceaneering International, Inc. Previously: President / Owner, Consilium C2C, LLC; and various management & leadership roles at Schlumberger for 20 years.

Michael Monahan, Agent, State Farm Insurance. Previously: Technical Sales Executive, Canon USA; Regional Sales Manager, Sun Microsystems, Branch Sales Manager, Sprint IT Consulting.

Lydon Neumann, Vice President, Impact Advisors. Previously: Senior Executive/Partner, Accenture LLP; Vice President, Cap Gemini Ernst & Young.

****Lucia Oddo**, Independent Management Consulting Professional. Previously: SVP Global Client Service, ACNielsen.

****John Osth**, CEO, NanoSomiX, Inc. Previously: President/CEO, Celula, Inc; President, Immunotherapy Div., Baxter Healthcare.

Greg Panagos, Investor relations executive. Previously: Senior Vice President, Investor Relations and Communications, Barrick Gold Corp; Vice President, Investor relations and Communications, Transocean Inc.; Director, Investor Relations, Noble Energy Inc.

Rick Pilgrim, President and Founder, QuickSilver Drilling Technologies. Previously: Vice President Engineering, LeTourneau Technologies; Manager Corporate Engineering, Ensco PLC.

****Patricia Recktenwald-Vasys**, Founder/CEO, Tech Buddys LLC. Previously: COO-Vice President, Sears Essentials, Sears Holdings Corporation; Vice President Operations, Northwest Region, Sears; Vice President Operations, Sears Hardware Stores.

Dianne Reece, Western Region Mgr., Organizational Development & Training, FMC Technologies, Subsea Systems. Previously: HR leadership positions, both domestic and international, for mid- to large-size global energy organizations.

John Robb, President, Tensetic Systems Inc. Previously: Vice President, FKP Architects, Inc.

Pam Rodgers, Talent Management & Development, WorleyParsons; Previously: Organization Effectiveness and Leadership Development positions in international professional and technology services companies.

Tacey A. Rosolowski, Ph.D., Manuscript Consultant and Writing Coach, Freelance since 1996. Sample clients: MD Anderson Cancer Center, Rice University, American Craft Magazine.

*Monica Rottman**, Vice President Human Resources, BorgWarner. Previously: Vice President Human Resources, Guardian Industries; Vice President Human Resources and Communications, Amcor.

Patrick Sandoval, Principal Project Manager, BG. Previously: Program Director, Worley-Parsons; Program Manager of Projects, WorleyParsons; Location Engineering Manager, Cairo, Egypt, WorleyParsons.

Art Saxby, CEO, Chief Outsiders. Previously: VP of Corporate Development, Sales & Marketing, Hines Horticulture; VP of Marketing, Imperial Sugar.

Larry Schwartz, NGL Fundamentals Advisor, British Petroleum. Previously: Senior Analyst NGL, Wood Mackenzie; Supply Optimization Group - Special Projects Advisor, Chevron.

Mark Schwartz, Senior Vice-President, Human Resources, Waste Management. Previously: VP & Assistant General Counsel, Waste Management, Inc.; Office Managing Shareholder, Littler Mendelson.

Richard Walsh, Executive and Leadership Coaching Consultant. Previously: SVP, Human Resources and Chief Administrative Officer, PerkinElmer, Inc; Guest Lecturer and Adjunct Faculty Member (2010/13), University of Houston, Bauer College of Business; SVP Human Resources, ABB, Inc.

John Wilson, Senior Vice President of Operations, Wilson Mohr.

Jason Zeller, Finance Director, Global Sales & Service, Weir Oil and Gas. Previous roles include: Chief Financial Officer (CFO), Cook Compression, A Dover Company; North American Operations Controller, GSE.

K. Dean Zipse, Executive Vice President, Marketing & Business Development, Big Eagle Services. Previously: Vice President, Marketing N.A., Bredero Shaw; Vice President, Sales & Operations, N.A., Flexpipe Systems.

FOREWORD

What percentage of organizational initiatives that you have observed over the past ten years have had a significant impact that lasted over 18 months?

The majority of executives in a recent survey, when asked this question, reported that fewer than 30% of the corporate initiatives were successful to this degree. I have asked this question hundreds of times in several decades of interviews, workshops and informal conversations and the median estimate always hovered around the 30% mark.

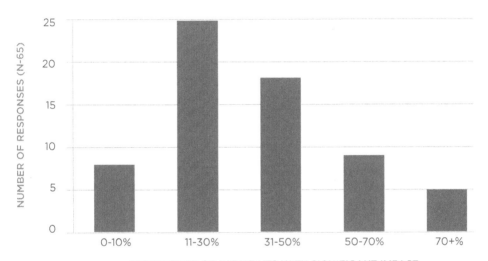

WHAT PERCENTAGE OF THE INITIATIVES YOU HAVE SEEN LAUNCHED OVER THE LAST TEN YEARS HAD A SIGNIFICANT IMPACT ON THE ORGANIZATION THAT LASTED FOR MORE THAN 18 MONTHS?

PERCENTAGE OF INITIATIVES WITH SIGNIFICANT IMPACT

What is most remarkable to me is, when I share this information in workshops and presentations, no one is surprised by this data. This means that this track record is accepted as a fact of life within most organizations. And this is the number given by executives who have launched these things! What would your front-line employees say about the impact of such initiatives? I can guarantee you, based on thirty years of consulting experience, their estimates will be a whole lot less than 30%!

The costs of these failed initiatives go far beyond the millions of dollars invested directly in them. They include the opportunity costs of misdirected resources and the decrease in credibility of the leadership who sponsored them—no one will take any initiatives seriously if they believe 70% of them will fail. In the Introduction Chapter, you will have an opportunity to calculate what a failed initiative costs your organization.

WHAT DO IDEAS HAVE TO DO WITH IT?
Leaders often overlook a key fact: an organizational initiative always starts with someone's idea for a different future. Once the idea is accepted as a good one, a project is usually

created to make that idea a reality. And here is where the problem starts: As soon as that project gets under way, the majority of the attention soon focuses on project tasks and deliverables, and the original idea of a different future gradually gets lost in the shuffle. In fact, it is often the case that such a project performs admirably and provides its deliverables on time and within budget and still yields no lasting business results. This is because the original idea was gradually changed from a picture of a new future for the organization to a list of project deliverables. This book deals with this challenge with a Four-Step Method for shepherding the idea behind the initiative through the organization—at the same time the initiative project team carries out its tasks and creates its deliverables. It also will point you in the right direction for delivering ideas through shorter-term processes such as meetings or even one-on-one conversations.

WHERE DO MY IDEAS ABOUT BUSINESS IDEAS COME FROM?

This book is about turning ideas into business results. It is based on interviews, surveys and direct observation of several hundred senior executives. Over the last 35 years I have consulted with a large variety of companies, from Fortune 500 companies to small start-ups and mid-sized firms. I have collaborated in a diversity of areas including project management, training development, organizational improvement, software design, strategic planning, and sales and marketing strategy. Most recently I have focused on coaching executives and their teams. Amid all of this diversity, I always had the sense that I was working on the same issues and applying the same skills no matter which of those activities I was supporting.

The commonality was this: These are all ways I helped my clients clarify their ideas of what they want to happen in the future and how to transform those ideas into business results. My hope is that this perspective, a perspective that focuses on the state of the idea—as opposed to the process or project that moves the idea through the organization—will provide you and other leaders with some new insights on why some ideas succeed and others fail.

About 20 years ago I began a systematic study of why the failure rate of initiatives is so high and what could be done about it. I started with a series of 1-hour interviews with 50 senior executives from approximately 25 organizations. The most significant finding was that the majority of such initiatives fail. Since that time, I have conducted hundreds of formal and informal interviews to further understand why that is the case and what executives can do to obtain a better track record.

Then, two years ago, I enlisted the help of more than 60 senior executives—some of whom had participated in my original study 20 years before. This executive panel agreed to review and provide input on the book's key concepts as I developed them. They did this through a series of on-line surveys, one-on-one conversations and a seminar. Many also reviewed drafts of individual chapters and even early drafts of the entire book. Their input confirmed that the success rate of organizational initiatives has not changed much in two decades. I now owe a debt of thanks to the clients and colleagues who have contributed to my thinking over these decades, only some of whom I have mentioned in the acknowledgements section. Because of their insights, and their willingness to experiment with the approaches described in this book, I have a much better understanding of the success factors that determine how ideas are turned into business results.

I gained an unexpected insight through this long-term investigation that expanded my thinking beyond that of organizational initiatives: The same principles that determine whether ideas succeed or fail in the context of organizational initiatives apply equally well to ideas delivered to the organization through a variety of other processes. For example, new product rollouts, sales campaigns, presentations to stockholders, and even meetings are all means of delivering ideas with the intention of a lasting impact. Even engineering projects with well-specified deliverables must also deliver important ideas about those deliverables and the company that provided them.

LEADING THROUGH IDEAS: A COMPETITIVE EDGE
The environment in which leaders currently compete is an environment of ideas, and this is an arena in which only the fittest ideas survive. Leaders need to fully understand the factors that determine how their ideas, and the ideas of their peers and employees, can turn into business results. This book describes how you can manage these success factors as well as assess and mitigate common risks ideas face as they are transformed from conception to results. Mastering the skills of leading through ideas will equip you to compete in this challenging environment of ideas.

INTRODUCTION
INITIATIVES THAT GO "POOF" IN THE NIGHT

INTRODUCTION
IN A NUTSHELL

Your role as a leader is to minimize the economic losses due to ineffective ideas by monitoring the health of ideas moving through your organization and managing the risks to their success.

KEY POINTS

- Ideas live in high risk, survival of the fittest environments. Idea risk management is an essential leadership skill.

- The Four-Step Method enables you to apply the concepts of idea leadership to specific ideas of your own, and you are encouraged to do so by completing the exercises found in Chapters 1 – 4.

- An idea becomes ineffective when more attention is given to the process that moves it forward, such as those associated with initiatives, than to the idea itself.

- Vetting an idea in terms of four characteristics will increase the probability of its success. These are:

    Focus: Clarity of the purpose of an idea, and of who needs to do what to make it happen.

    Shape: The contour and texture of an idea determines the efficiency with which it moves through the organization.

    Alignment. The relationship of an idea to other ideas within the organization has a significant effect on its momentum.

    Engagement. The degree to which an idea engages the hearts, as well as the minds, of the people who will implement an idea determines how much of themselves they will invest in it.

WHY DO INITIATIVES GO "POOF" IN THE NIGHT?

I frequently use the following story to begin interviews and conversations about corporate initiatives, and it always prompts a telling response:

The executive team of a mid-market manufacturing company attended its annual weekend retreat and came up with ten strategic ideas that they then launched with ten strategic initiatives. Nine months later, the Chairman asked the CEO about their status:

CHAIRMAN: "Do you recall those initiatives you all put together last year?"

CEO: "Oh yeah—darn good initiatives, those were! Darn good!"

CHAIR: "Whatever happened to them?"

CEO: "We remain committed to them all."

CHAIR: "What's the status? What kind of outcomes have you seen?"

CEO: "They are coming along well. Good impact."

When senior executives hear this story, they give a wry smile of guilty recognition. When I tell it to lower level managers or employees, I tend to get a guffaw, often with comments like "Oh yea, the flavor of the month;" or "Those of us who have been around for a while have learned to duck our heads when the pendulum flies by—it's just a matter of time before it swings back in the other direction." They simply avoid the initiative as best they can, waiting for the inevitable "poof."

The knowing grimaces and guffaws I've seen in interviews over the years reflect the general belief that corporate initiatives fail more often than not. These failures are expensive. To get an estimate of the financial impact of failed initiatives in your organization, take a couple of minutes to do the following, using conservative seat-of-the-pants estimates:

1. **Jot down a quick list of ten corporate initiatives with which you have been involved over the past several years.** Depending on the size of your organization, an initiative might be as broad as unifying your corporate culture or as narrow as rolling out a new product or service to your customers, or establishing a new approach to performance management.

2. **Estimate the number of full time equivalents (FTE) required to plan, communicate and implement each initiative.** Be sure to include the less obvious employee time consumed by distractions, learning curves and other inefficiencies of change.

3. **Multiply the FTE by average salaries and total the results.** Be sure to include an appropriate share of overhead expenses.

4. **Add costs for consultants and other contractors.**

5. **Add cost of missed opportunities.** This includes the normal sales, product development and other activities forgone in the pursuit of the initiatives.

Whatever number you come up with, no matter how conservative the estimates, you will see that it is very high. This book will help you significantly reduce these costs.

The Impact Of Ideas On Employees

Employees act only on the ideas they have in their own heads. If they don't share your idea, whether presented as a policy or procedure or rolled out through a large scale initiative, they will not act on it as you hope they will. No matter how well-defined the idea is on paper or in PowerPoint presentations, if that idea is not understood and accepted into the minds—and the hearts—of employees, it will be a failure. This is as true for your direct reports as it is for your front-line workers.

Your ideas succeed or fail because of how other people think of them, how they picture them in their own minds and, then, how they act on them. If you think that an idea for a different future will work because it works in your mind, but you don't understand how it will work in the minds of your employees or other stakeholders, then it is at a high risk of failure. This is true whether the time scale for that future is in years, as in the case of many initiatives, or in minutes, as when you delegate a task to a subordinate or present an idea to a customer.

This is why I frequently refer to how ideas work in an organizational environment rather than how initiatives work. An initiative usually consists of a variety of projects and/or processes designed to deliver an idea to the organization. For example, a typical initiative might include some sort of roll-out process, training programs, performance management systems, communication strategies and the like—and they are often wrapped into an overall project plan. Managing these processes is extremely important because they move ideas from conception to results. But, it is equally important to keep track of and manage the original idea so that it doesn't become lost in these processes or turn into something that doesn't deliver the changes you envision. You don't want to be in the position where the operation was a success but you lost the patient.

Processes Vs. Ideas –
A Critical Difference

In order for a leader to have the impact she wants, she must know how to lead her organization with an idea from the moment that idea is conceived to the final stages when the idea achieves the intended business results. This is a complex activity taking place over time. In order to be able to control what happens and lead effectively, a leader must pay attention to the distinction between the idea she wishes to deliver to the organization and the processes by which she delivers it. An initiative—with its various supporting processes—is merely the engine that transports an idea conceived in one part of the organization to those who can transform it into on-the-ground results. The most common reason that ideas fail to achieve the intended results is that, once that engine is set into motion, the majority of the attention gets focused on the engine while the original idea itself gets lost—it goes poof. When that happens, people scratch their heads and ask, "What purpose is this engine serving? Why do we keep it running?" Since no one knows for sure, it is often let alone and sooner or later it runs out of gas. Or, if it has gotten to be an encumbrance to the organization, or an embarrassment, it will be shunted off into a siding, derailed or even blown up.

Organizational initiatives are not the only way leaders move ideas from conception to results. Sometimes these undertakings are called "projects" or "ventures." Other idea-moving processes range from strategic planning to training programs to one-on-one performance feedback sessions. I focus on organizational initiatives in this book because they usually attract a lot of attention and people more readily notice their successes and failures. In addition, the lessons learned from studying organizational initiatives are easily transferred to other idea delivery processes.

Throughout my discussion of ideas, I will show you how to keep your focus on what happens to ideas as they are moved forward by initiatives and other processes. Our focus will not be on the processes themselves. There are many books and training programs about processes for making change happen. Topics include project management, change management, sales at the individual and enterprise level, problem solving, business process improvement, and the list goes on. I have authored and taught many of these myself. While none of these processes are implemented for their own sake, this seemingly obvious point is often forgotten. Their purpose is to carry an idea from its initial conception to the business results envisioned for the future. The big idea of a project is not the deliverable—the big idea is how and why the deliverable will be used to achieve business results.

When An Idea Gets Lost In The Process Intended To Deliver It

The reason these idea delivery mechanisms sometimes fail to achieve the desired results is that the original idea becomes lost in the process. The example below shows how this can happen in a project environment.

THE IDEA OF THE DELIGHTFUL BUYING EXPERIENCE

THE ORIGINAL IDEA
Forrest, the SVP for on-line retail sales had an idea. He called it "The Delightful Buying Experience." He described his idea to his staff as follows: "I see the customer opening up the home page, immediately finding what she wants and purchasing it with a single click with absolutely no distractions or confusion. Most of all, I want customers to be delighted as they leave the site." His staff all agreed that this was an excellent idea.

CREATING THE PROCESS TO CARRY FORWARD THE IDEA
Forrest appointed a staff member from retail sales to meet with a representative of the internal IT group to outline a project to carry out the idea of The Delightful Buying Experience. After extensive deliberations, they agreed on a detailed list of specifications for the end product, along with resource allocations and a timeline. The software project manager was adamant that Forrest sign off on all specifications, because she "wanted to deliver the project on time, on budget and conforming exactly to the idea Forrest had in mind."

EXECUTING THE PROCESS TO CARRY FORWARD THE IDEA

The project manager was eager for this important project to be a success, so she insisted that her software team members be assigned full time to her project and that they all work within the same enclosed office space to ensure a high degree of collaboration and to insulate the team from distractions. She told her team, "I don't want you thinking about anything but meeting those specifications within time and budget."

THE DELIVERY OF THE SOFTWARE INTENDED TO CARRY FORWARD THE IDEA

The project manager drove her team hard and delivered the software exactly to specifications, on time and within budget. The software team and the retail team met to celebrate their achievement, and the SVP congratulated them for a job well done.

THE IDEA OF THE DELIGHTFUL BUYING EXPERIENCE AS IMPLEMENTED

The customers were not delighted as originally conceived by the SVP, once the idea was actually implemented. Even though customers were able to have a single-click experience without distractions, customers no longer were prompted with suggestions for related products and they found it more difficult to browse through the site to find them. The younger generations complained that the site was boring. The process was executed perfectly and met all specifications. However, the original idea of The Delightful Buying Experience had fallen by the wayside.

It is not unusual for the idea behind a project to get lost in the shuffle of project activities— participants get so interested in the project process that they forget to pay attention to the idea. The same thing often happens as other processes are executed to move ideas from conception to results. Think of off-site meetings held to move forward key ideas where the event was well-executed but led to no meaningful results. Think of ideas you have delegated to others that emerged from the execution process very differently than you hoped for. Think of bureaucracies that have collapsed under their own weight because more attention was given to maintaining the processes originally created to carry out good ideas than to those original ideas themselves.

I do not want to imply that ideas shouldn't change as others carry them forward but, rather, that these changes should occur purposefully and not accidentally. It is the job of the leader to keep track of the state of ideas as they move from conception to results to ensure that such changes are deliberate and appropriate. It is also the job of the leader to anticipate and mitigate the risks ideas encounter as they are moved forward by these processes.

When Ideas Go "Poof"

The example of the Delightful Buying Experience illustrates how an idea can fail even though the delivery process is given constant, focused attention. As you will see in Chapter 1, ideas most often fail to achieve their intended results not because of anyone's overt actions, but because the ideas slowly die from inattention and neglect.

Based on my research and hands-on observations of processes intended to move ideas from conception to results, I now understand why ideas go "poof" in the night. Ideas disappear into thin air when they fail to make the journey from the imaginations of their originators—whether leaders or their employees—into the minds and hearts of those required to support and implement the idea.

All organizations have thousands if not millions of ideas floating through them. Because of this, any single idea exists in a high-risk, survival-of-the-fittest environment. When you hand off an idea for implementation by other people in the organization, they need to understand from their own perspectives why it is important to them as well as to the organization. If they don't feel that your idea for the future is meaningful to them, they will put their energy behind something else that is. Your idea will fail to gain the necessary momentum and have little chance of achieving the impact you desire.

To ensure that your idea is shared by others in a way that yields meaningful results, you must attend to two broad concerns: First, you need to understand how different types of ideas behave in the organizational environment so you can take the steps required for your ideas to gather momentum and have the impact you intend. Second, you must understand the risks your ideas face in the organizational environment over the short and long terms. You can then increase the probability of the success of your ideas by assessing, monitoring and mitigating those risks.

What Kinds Of Ideas Am I Talking About

Because ideas come in all sizes and shapes, I would like to clarify what I am and am not talking about when I refer to "ideas." To set the stage, I would like to identify five types of ideas found within organizations, defined primarily by their time horizons.

TYPE OF IDEA	TIME FRAME
Future Vision	Over 5 years
Strategic ideas	1-5 years
Tactical ideas	1-12 months
Immediate ideas	Less than a week
Foundational Beliefs	Enduring

Throughout the chapters, I will focus primarily on Immediate, Tactical, and Strategic ideas and their role in moving the organization toward its Future Vision. However as a leader, you must also remain aware of how Foundational Beliefs can either support or resist these ideas. This book does not deal directly with the generation of ideas but, rather, what to do with them after they are generated. Let me briefly expand the definitions of each of the five types of ideas.

> **The Future Vision** serves as a beacon for all of the Strategic, Tactical and Immediate Ideas in the organization. To the extent these ideas are aimed in the direction of the same Future Vision, they will be able to capitalize on each other's momentum.

Strategic Ideas are carried forward by large scale processes sometimes called "strategic initiatives," usually with substantial executive support. They are tied to a well-defined future vision toward which a leader guides her organization. As you have seen, in spite of such substantial investments, the executives I have interviewed tell me strategic ideas fail to achieve a significant impact more often than not.

Tactical Ideas are carried forward with short-term projects, programs or assignments. Ideally, they directly support Strategic Ideas and the Future Vision. Unfortunately, Tactical Ideas often are not aligned with either the Strategic Ideas or the Future Vision because of more pressing realities such as this quarter's deliverables and unexpected crises that demand immediate attention.

Immediate Ideas may run from conception to results in as little as an hour—they are moved forward by very short-term processes such as sales calls, presentations, meetings or even focused conversations. Most people, even senior executives, do not consciously consider their Future Vision as they carry out these every-day processes that move their ideas along. However, as an aggregate, far more time and thought probably are expended on the Immediate Ideas within an organization than all the Strategic and Tactical Ideas combined.

Foundational Beliefs are the traditional core cultural assumptions and values of the organization that provide its strength and stability. At the same time, their gravitational pull can drag new ideas out of alignment with the targeted Future Vision.

Many people will find the most immediate practical application of this book is to increase the success rate of strategic ideas carried forward by large scale organizational initiatives. However, you will find that the principles and practical suggestions you will read about apply equally well to ideas with shorter-term impacts—the tactical and immediate ideas. I will use examples of ideas delivered through organizational initiatives quite a bit to help make these concepts concrete. However, I will also encourage you to think about the book's utility in increasing the success rate of all sorts of ideas delivered by all sorts of processes, whether you call these processes conversations, meetings, projects, or strategic initiatives. Most of all, this is a practical book about ideas that will help you to answer the question: "What can I do to increase the success rate of ideas in which my organization invests?"

Turning Good Ideas Into Ideas That Work

Initiatives don't fail primarily because they are based on bad ideas. Most people I interviewed found it very easy to identify initiatives that met an untimely death even though, they felt, the ideas behind them were sound. There were also many examples of initiatives based on obviously bad ideas that hung around the organization—perhaps in the form of ineffective policies or procedures—and continued to have negative impacts, in spite of the fact that many people recognized the basic ideas as ineffective or even counterproductive. While an initiative based on a good idea (whatever "good" means in a particular context), has a higher chance of survival than one based on a bad idea, starting off with a good idea is not sufficient, or even necessary, for its survival.

My research has identified characteristics of ideas other than their intrinsic worth that determine their longevity, whether the processes used to carry them forward take the form of large scale initiatives or short-term meetings. In the chapters that follow, I will share with you what I have learned. Throughout, I will provide some practical tips on how to build in the Success Factors and mitigate the most common risks. If you are a leader of an organization or team, these insights will help you to monitor and manage the forward movement of your ideas—and the ideas of others—so that, instead of going "poof," they will take on weight, substance and power, and achieve the impact you desire. If you are one who leads without the title of an executive or even manager, you will learn how to how to influence change in your organization without that formal authority. This book will also help you to help others make their ideas successful. You will find out how to turn good ideas into ideas that work. You will learn to lead through ideas. The book is organized into two parts:

- Part I: The Four-Step Method
- Part II: Extending the Four-Step Method Beyond Organizational Initiatives

Overview Of Part I: The Four-Step Method

Any idea introduced to an organization lives in a high risk environment—if this weren't so, initiatives and other processes used to move ideas forward would have a much higher success rate.

Through the analysis of my interview data I have identified the following four factors that affect the success of any idea.

- Focus
- Shape
- Alignment
- Engagement

These four factors are relevant whether your idea is launched through a brief comment in a meeting or a formal rollout of a large corporate initiative. They form the basis of the Four-Step Method.

STEP 1
FOCUS YOUR IDEA FOR IMPACT.

⬇

STEP 2
SHAPE YOUR IDEA FOR UNDERSTANDING.

⬇

STEP 3
ALIGN YOUR IDEA FOR SYNERGY.

⬇

STEP 4
ENGAGE YOUR IDEA FOR COMMITMENT.

Step 1 – Focus Your Idea for Impact. Focus describes the degree to which your idea is directed toward a specific targeted Purpose and the clarity with which you and others understand exactly who must take what actions to achieve that purpose. An inadequate Focus will cause your idea to land off target, squandering scarce resources and limiting the impact of your idea. Focus is the topic of Chapter 1.

Step 2 – Shape Your Idea for Understanding. The Shape of your idea—its contour and texture—affects how it moves through the environment and impacts its target, almost as if it were a physical object. For example, a very pointed idea is sometimes necessary to move people to action, while a less well-defined idea may offer more flexibility to those charged with implementing it. Shape is the topic of Chapter 2.

Step 3 – Align Your Idea for Synergy. Aligning your idea with other ideas in the environment enables you to leverage the energy that already exists in the organization. This avoids having your Idea dragged down or off course by ideas that have acquired negative connotations or are simply moving in the wrong direction. Careful planning may enable you to take advantage of the momentum of ideas moving in the same direction. When you leave these matters to chance, you risk missing opportunities to conserve resources through piggy-backing or wasting resources through unexpected conflict. Alignment is the topic of Chapter 3.

Step 4 – Engage Your Idea for Commitment. The success of your idea depends substantially on the degree to which it has engaged the hearts, as well as the minds, of the people whose support you need for its successful implementation. If no one cares, no one will act—and the momentum of your idea will be wasted. You can minimize the associated risks through an analysis of how your idea is perceived through the various lenses each stakeholder habitually uses. Engagement is the topic of Chapter 4.

The Structure Of Chapters 1 - 4

Each of these chapters is designed to help you to apply one of these steps to an idea of your own, and is organized as follows:

In a Nutshell: A very brief overview of the key concepts of the chapter.

Put Your Stake in the Ground: At the start of each chapter, you will be asked to identify a specific idea of yours to encourage you to apply what you read in that chapter to a situation of your own.

How Ideas Work: The first half of each chapter describes in detail how its respective factor affects the success of ideas with substantial detailed examples to illustrate the major concepts.

Your Turn: The second half of each chapter puts you in the driver's seat. The first thing you will do is evaluate the idea you identified at the beginning of the chapter using the framework you just read about.

Success Factor Analysis: You will then be introduced to five success factors related to this step, and you will evaluate your idea in terms of each.

Risk Factor Analysis: Likewise, you will be introduced to five risk factors, and you will identify those that pose the greatest risk to your idea so that you can develop a risk mitigation approach.

Questions to Start a Conversation: Finally, each chapter ends with a list of questions you can use to involve your people in the thought processes introduced in that chapter.

Now What? This brief section merely asks you to identify some specific actions you will take to strengthen the success factors and reduce the risk factors.

Overview of Part II:
Extending The Four-Step Method Beyond Organizational Initiatives

The final portion of the book extends to application of the Four-Step Method to ideas beyond those typically delivered by initiatives but that are critically important to leadership success.

Chapter 5, "The Idea of The-Organization-You-Lead" demonstrates how to apply the method to the idea of your own organization. You will follow a case study that demonstrates each step of the method and you will be asked to assess the Purpose, Shape, Alignment and Engagement of the idea people have in their heads when your organization comes to mind, and to make the necessary adjustments for that idea to have the impact you intend.

Chapter 6, "The Idea of You-as-Leader" applies the same Four-Step Method, supported by a case study, to the idea of yourself that you project to your organization. As in Chapter 5, you will be asked to assess and develop the idea of You-as-Leader to increase the effective use of your role to achieve the results you intend.

Chapter 7, "Balancing Tensions Among Ideas" describes the challenge anyone who leads through ideas faces as they encounter the tensions between the way they would like things to be and the way they are. This is illustrated in a brief case study of the culture at Arthur Andersen from approximately 1980 through its demise in 2002.

How To Read This Book

A cover-to-cover read will allow chapters to build on one another and give you a comprehensive understanding of idea processes and effective leadership strategies.

Jump to the numbered success and risk factors if you need very practical information to maximize the probability of success of an idea. The second part of each of the next four chapters provides practical details on the success factors covered in that chapter as well as the risk factors associated with it.

Start a conversation using lists of questions at the end of each chapter if you need to engage others in the process of planning for the success and mitigating risks of ideas. These questions can also help raise your awareness about how to ensure the success and manage the risks faced by your ideas and the ideas of others.

Skip to the Appendix to get a global picture. I summarize both the success and risk factors in single checklists as a useful reference. The appendix also groups in one place the planning tools illustrated elsewhere in the book. Glancing over it may give you a sense of the book's content. It will also help you to understand how to apply the Four-Step Method to contexts other than corporate initiatives, such as project management, communications, coaching and organizational development.

However you choose to approach this book, I encourage you to think of very specific examples you have faced or are facing as you or your people transform good ideas into ideas that work. This will provide you with the greatest return on the investment of the time you spend with this book.

PART I
THE FOUR-STEP METHOD

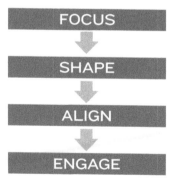

CHAPTER 1
Focus Your Idea
for Impact

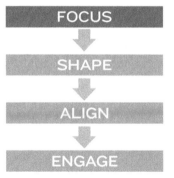

FOCUS

SHAPE

ALIGN

ENGAGE

STEP 1: FOCUS
IN A NUTSHELL

Your role as a leader is to Focus your idea by making certain that people are absolutely clear on who is expected to take what actions, and why—so that ideas achieve the maximum impact with the least expenditure of resources.

KEY POINTS

- When you focus an idea, you ensure that its momentum is directed where it will have the greatest impact. This requires defining its:

  Purpose: The strategic rationale for the idea as well as its immediate objectives.

  Actors: The specific individuals who will act on the idea.

  Actions: The specific actions those individuals will take.

- Neglecting one or more of these components increases the likelihood that your idea will degenerate into one of the following four types of ineffective ideas:

  An Inert Idea: A fine sounding idea with an admirable purpose on which no one takes any sort of action.

  A Lonely Idea: An idea with a clear purpose and well-defined actions but which everyone avoids.

  A Busy Idea: An idea that results in many people taking many actions, without anyone understanding why.

  An Immobilized Idea: An idea to which all are committed but on which no one takes any action.

- The Idea Impact Matrix is a tool that enables you to focus the momentum of an idea by identifying a few representative individuals and the specific actions each will take to achieve its defined purpose.

BEFORE YOU START THIS CHAPTER:
PUT YOUR STAKE IN THE GROUND

EXERCISE

The purpose of this very brief exercise, found at the beginning of each of Chapters 1-4, is to encourage you to apply what you read in each chapter to a situation of your own.

Describe how you refer to your idea:

_____

Give a short name or phrase you would use in normal conversation when discussing this idea. For example, it might be a single word, such as "Quality" or "Excellence," or a phrase such as "Increasing shareholder value through employee commitment."

Identify the 2-3 processes you will use or (have used / are using) to deliver this idea to the organization:

_____

_____

You will find it most useful if you can identify 2-3 more specific processes, such as:

- *"A series of cascading meetings from senior executives down to front-line personnel."*
- *"A training program to introduce the idea, clarify its importance, and identify new related policies and procedures."*
- *"An on-going communication program with posters, e-mails, teleconferences and executive updates."*

THE MOMENTUM OF AN IDEA

Suppose you want to knock over an empty ten gallon bucket from ten or fifteen feet away. Think of throwing a handful of gravel at it, as compared to throwing a rock at the same velocity and of the same total mass. If you throw the gravel, it will cover a broad path, and those pebbles that happen to hit the can may make an impressive amount of noise; however, their combined impact will be minimal because most of the stones will have missed the target. If you throw the rock, you will probably knock the bucket over, especially if you aim directly at the top center. You achieve your desired impact because the energy you use to throw the rock is focused where it makes the biggest difference.

The same principle applies to an idea. The more you can focus its momentum on a defined target, the more effective impact it will have. A young company with a new product often makes the mistake of spreading its marketing and sales resources as broadly as possible. They throw their ideas at as many people as they can with the hope of having an impact on some potential customer. The result is that no one buys their product because each potential customer gets hit with only a pebble or two. The founders of such a company do this in an attempt to maximize the impact of their limited resources. However, it is usually more effective for them to identify a few target markets with the highest potential for finding the product useful, and aim its concentrated resources directly at those.

I would like to reinforce here a point that every sales or marketing person knows but is easy to forget: the customer rarely buys a product but, rather, buys the idea of the product that is presented to him. Thus, the function of the sales process is to deliver the idea to the customer in the hope that he will take the action of signing on the dotted line. Only when the customer accepts delivery of the idea of the product will he take that desired action.

This basic premise is fundamental to all discussions in this book—that an individual will take action in response to an idea only if he first accepts delivery of the idea. It applies to an idea delivered to employees through the process of an organizational initiative as well as to an idea delivered to a potential customer through a sales process.

It is sometimes difficult for people to tighten the focus of the idea they are delivering because they are afraid of missing out on opportunities. You may make the same mistake anytime you give a presentation, prepare for a meeting, interview for a new position—or promote an idea through a corporate initiative. If you try to be all things to all people, you risk having a significant impact on none. The best approach is to think carefully about where you want to have an impact and design your ideas accordingly. This chapter describes that thought process.

THREE REQUIREMENTS FOR A FOCUSED IDEA

The three components required for an idea to achieve an impact are so obvious that leaders rarely spend enough time thinking about them: 1) an idea needs to be translated into actions for it to make a difference; 2) actions need an actor to carry them out; and, 3) actions taken without some kind of purpose are a waste of resources.

REQUIREMENTS FOR A FOCUSED IDEA

When you, as a leader, launch an idea through the process of an organizational initiative—or you help others to do so—it is useful to think in a disciplined way about three questions:

- What is the Purpose of the idea?
- Who (what Actor) do I want to take action as a result of this idea?
- Exactly what Action do I want that actor to take?

The Executive Review Panel responses to a survey indicate that the creators of the failed initiatives with which they were familiar frequently lacked clarity on one or more on these three requirements. While 43 of the 64 panel members who responded to this item believed the business purpose of the failed initiatives had been clear to its creators the majority of the time, only 29 thought the initiatives' creators had been clear about who was required to take the appropriate actions. Only 19 believed they had been clear about what actions were required.

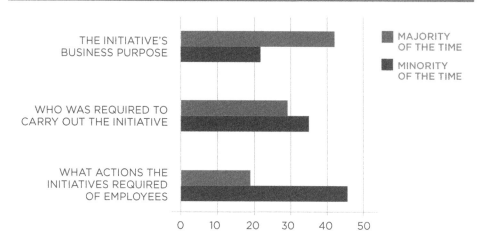

The Executive Review Panel further reported that the employees who were expected to carry out the failed initiatives had been even less clear than the initiatives' creators about these three factors. Only 23 of the 64 believed that, for the majority of these initiatives, the employees who were expected to carry them out could have explained its business purpose. Similarly, only 13 believed that employees had been held accountable for their actions and results, and only 19 thought that the employees had been aware of their employer's expectations of them the majority of the time.

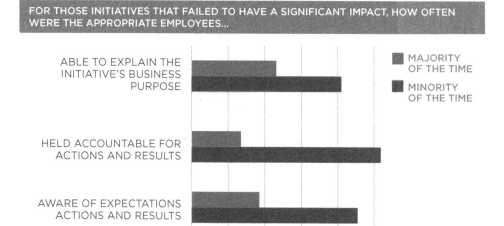

The lack of clarity about the three factors of Purpose, Actor and Action among both the creators of the failed initiatives and the employees who were expected to carry them out provide some insight into the potential causes of their failures.

DEFINING PURPOSE,
ACTOR AND ACTION

The following discussion of Purpose, Actor and Action is based on an actual situation I faced with a client, as described in the accompanying example. The details of this and most other examples in this book have been altered for simplicity and to protect the client's identity.

THE IDEA OF COLLABORATION IN A SOFTWARE COMPANY

Since its inception 40 years ago, a major software firm considered collegial collaboration among engineers to be one of its core values. However, the current SVP for research felt that the idea of collaboration being critical to their success was fading into the background, as teams became more globally dispersed and interacted virtually. He felt that the diminished level of concern for collaboration increased cross-border communication errors that, in turn, led to increased time-to-market of new products and a decrease in quality.

Senior executives had tried in the past to restore collaboration through a variety of initiatives, but with little success. While people generally thought increased collaboration would be a very good thing, the impact of those initiatives had been minimal because no one knew how they were expected to turn the warm and fuzzy idea of Collaboration into actions that made a difference. This time around, we assembled a team to think through collaboration in a more disciplined way. The following text describes the details of how we did this.

CLARIFYING THE PURPOSE

I worked with the team to help them define exactly what they wanted to achieve by promoting the idea of Collaboration, i.e., what purpose it was to serve. I explained that the purpose of an idea is defined, in part, by its most immediate objective—what change is expected as a direct result of promoting the idea. More significantly, I explained, the purpose of an idea describes why that change is important to the organization in the longer term. The purpose of an idea should specify how achieving its immediate objective will move the organization toward its vision, or how it will move other tactical or strategic ideas in that direction.

In the case of the above example, the team determined that the immediate purpose of promoting the idea of Collaboration was fewer errors due to miscommunication during software handoffs between regions. They also identified that the longer-term purpose of the idea—why this change matters—is that collaboration would support the strategic goal of beating the competition to market on software innovations while maintaining quality. When a leader thinks through the purpose of an idea she is promoting, she must ask "Why?" and then, perhaps, ask "Why?" several times more. For instance, in the current example, the initiative team answered these successive "Why's" with responses such as "...because we need to increase market share" and then "...because our stockholders are losing faith in our ability to compete," and so forth.

One of the reasons the most recent effort to improve collaboration made little difference was that the executives who launched that initiative did so without clearly defining either the immediate objectives or the longer term purpose of promoting the idea of Collaboration. They felt the value of collaboration was self evident and, thus, didn't require much discussion. As a result, this important idea, which they rolled out through a process they called "The Collaboration Initiative," quickly dissipated. Without adequate Focus, no one within the software development teams knew what the executives were trying to accomplish, or why.

You will significantly improve the impact of an idea important to you when you spend some extra time thinking through and discussing its immediate and long-term purposes. This will help ensure that your resources are focused exactly where they will provide you the biggest bang for your buck.

CLARIFYING THE ACTORS

The second component necessary for an idea to be focused is a specification of the Actors, i.e., "exactly who is required to take some action on this idea to achieve the intended results?" The question may not be as easy to answer as it first appears, because different groups may need to take different actions.

The software company in pursuit of collaboration had a reputation for knee-jerk reactions to problems. In their initial attempt to roll out the Collaboration Initiative, they didn't take the time necessary to involve the appropriate members of the software group in defining the idea of Collaboration, to allow them to take ownership of it and to experiment with it. Neither did they provide any practical guidance on how to actually integrate the idea of Collaboration into their day-to-day activities and relationships. They merely carried out a process, the Collaboration Initiative, consisting of events such as video broadcasts by leadership, reminder emails, posters and contests. Almost from the start, the process of the initiative separated itself from the idea it was intended to move forward—if they were ever connected in the first place. While employees recognized that the leadership had launched an initiative to promote collaboration, they made no changes in how they did their work.

When the Collaboration Initiative was launched the first time, the initiative team generally expected that those involved with global product development would understand the concept of collaboration and do what was necessary to increase their level of collaboration. The problem was that these were expectations they had of employees in general, not of specific individuals. While people in the global production group each had some idea of what was meant by collaboration, they did not have a clear idea of how it applied to them as individuals. The result was a nice sounding and well-intentioned idea that had no practical impact.

This time around, before any initiative process was even planned, the SVP of product development pushed his staff to be quite clear about exactly who needed to think differently about the idea of Collaboration—and how they were to act differently. In reality, effective collaboration requires the involvement of a large number of people in different roles. However, to focus their thinking, the collaboration team narrowed its attention to just three principal groups of actors. They focused on product managers, who were responsible for the overall success of the software products; product group leaders, who were responsible for designing and developing individual product components; and product team members, who were responsible for carrying out specific software-related tasks. Having identified the principle actors, they were then ready to describe the actions expected of each of these three groups of people—and communicate the appropriate messages to each of them.

When you promote an idea, whether through the process of a brief presentation or a long-term initiative, identifying the specific people who you most want to act on your idea will help you to target your message directly at them rather than at a general group. Remember: general expectations of everyone often are interpreted by individuals as general expectations of everyone else.

CLARIFYING THE ACTIONS

The actions required from each group of actors comprise the third component needing to be clarified for an idea to achieve its desired impact. The desired action can be as simple as wanting a customer to say "yes" to your proposal. Usually, however, the situation is more complicated. For example, exactly what action do you want someone to take in response to your idea of Organizational Safety? Do you want top executives to mention it in every meeting or, perhaps, demonstrate support for the idea through their own behaviors? Do you want plant managers to help their employees understand how safety relates to their family's security? Do you want HR to build an employee's safety record into his compensation calculations? Or, do you simply want employees to observe basic safety rules? Of course, the action you want depends on the actor you are thinking about, and you may want each of these actions to be taken. But, given an hour, you and your staff could think up literally hundreds of possible actions as well as actors. Focusing on them all would be futile. But, I can guarantee that the discussions your team has while narrowing the list to less than a dozen actions would significantly sharpen their thoughts on what the idea of Organizational Safety actually means in your situation and what behaviors you expect from promoting that idea.

It may seem like a tall order to narrow down the actions required of employees in a large organization to a small number and still have the idea be meaningful. But many companies have done just that. For example, those in the petroleum industry do take safety extremely seriously. I know a large company that has narrowed its idea about safety to a single action. They require that every single meeting in the company begin with a "safety moment," in which at least a minute must be devoted to some topic of safety. This action is implemented consistently from project team meetings to board meetings. The reason they have been able to maintain this degree of compliance is that they have narrowed the concept to a single and fairly simple action. Of course, this same company has literally thousands of pages of safety rules and regulations as well. But the "safety moment" strategically focuses the idea of Organizational Safety into one universal action that will promote adherence to all the rules. Because of the idea of Organizational Safety is focused on a clearly defined action, it has a more significant total impact on employee awareness of safety as a core value than any number of team posters, training programs or roll-out extravaganzas could ever have.

When you take the time to define the actions you expect people to take as a result of your idea, it is less likely to dissipate in the process of moving it forward, and you are more likely to achieve the results you envision.

THE IDEA IMPACT MATRIX

The software company executives who previously sought to promote the idea of Collaboration—through the process of their Collaboration Initiative—failed because they neglected to focus their idea of Collaboration. They neglected to clarify in their own minds the short and long-term purposes of promoting the idea of Collaboration, as well as the actors and actions required to achieve those purposes. Because the term "collaboration" was frequently used to describe the company's historical roots, executives and their product managers felt that the idea of Collaboration didn't need to be further defined. They felt it had a common sense meaning that everyone could be expected to understand. The problem was that, while everyone had a general sense of what collaboration meant, each had their own ideas about how it translated into specific behaviors. Because of this, the executives could not have meaningful discussions with each other about the initiative process by which the idea would be delivered to the organization. Nor could they discuss their expectations of, or their progress toward, increased collaboration. It was likewise impossible for the product managers to provide meaningful feedback to employees about the quality of their collaboration. These are important reasons why the previous Collaboration Initiative never had an impact.

This time, the collaboration team spent several hours around a white board forcing each other to be quite specific and practical about how the idea of Collaboration would be translated into action during each phase of the initiative process. Initially there was little agreement. However, the discussion helped them to sharpen their own ideas and come to a consensus about exactly what changes would most likely achieve the impact they were looking for. The results of this discussion about expected actions, and the previous one that defined the actors, are shown in an Idea Impact Matrix. This matrix also lists different behaviors identified for each stage of the process they referred to as "The New Collaboration Initiative." The clarity of this matrix provided a framework that focused subsequent discussions to refine the idea of Collaboration in even greater practical detail, and to create a plan to sustain that idea over the long term.

IDEA IMPACT MATRIX

What is the desired result of this idea, and who is expected to do what and when, to achieve that result?

THE IDEA: Collaboration   **THE PROCESS:** The New Collaboration Initiative

LONG-TERM PURPOSE: Increase quality, be first-to-market with our products

IMMEDIATE OBJECTIVE: Fewer errors due to miscommunications when software under development is handed off from region to region, around the globe and around the clock.

	THE ACTIONS		
THE ACTORS	**2 MONTHS**	**3 MONTHS**	**4-6 MONTHS**
PRODUCT MANAGERS	Agree there is a collaboration problem Agree on nature of problem Verbal commitment to solve the problem	Define standards of collaboration Get buy-in from direct reports Define metrics	Monitor metrics Provide regular on-the-job coaching Draw attention of teams to situations when collaboration made a difference
PRODUCT TEAM LEADERS	Withhold judgment that this is just another "knee-jerk response"	Provide honest feedback to product managers on the approach Examine own role in collaboration problems Get buy-in from direct reports Communicate metrics	Demonstrate collaboration across teams Include collaboration metrics in project updates
PRODUCT TEAM MEMBERS	Remain focused on normal operations Withhold judgment on rumors of changes	Translate expected behaviors and metrics into practical team standards	Demonstrate collaboration behaviors in practical ways that impact results.

WHEN A REQUIREMENT FOR FOCUS IS MISSING

An idea will fail to have an impact if any one of the three requirements for a focused idea is missing. It doesn't matter if it is the Action, the Actor or the Purpose. If one or more is missing, the idea will lose momentum and turn into one of the following forms as it is moved forward by an initiative, a project or some other process:

- An Inert Idea
- A Lonely Idea
- A Busy Idea
- An Immobilized Idea

Each of these forms has distinct characteristics. Understanding them will help you to recognize them when you see them, and to design your ideas to achieve the impact you intend.

INERT IDEAS

An Inert Idea has a clear purpose but the actors and the actions required to achieve it are fuzzy and undefined. Ideas labeled "Quality," or "Continuous Improvement," or "Excellence"—all fine ideas of the last several decades—very quickly became inert in many organizations. Inert Ideas are sometimes born when a senior executive reads a book (like this one!) on the airplane and sends an email to a direct report with instructions to implement it. Sources of Inert Ideas are varied. Some may emerge from the grandiose hopes and dreams of a corporate leader that never go beyond vague ambiguities. Others may reflect culturally-imbedded beliefs and values from the past that have lost their meaning through rote repetition. Such ideas are often expressed in lofty and all-encompassing words or phrases by well-intentioned executives to describe their organization's mission, vision or values. These leaders may imagine that such ideas define the essence of their organization, their guiding principles, their core culture or their reason for being—in short, their purpose. However, despite noble intentions, these ideas are often no more than window dressing, cynically tagged by employees as the "flavor of the month" or more simply as "corporate B.S." This is because no one actually understands the espoused purpose in terms concrete enough to provide a foundation for action, much less develop any sense of commitment to the idea.

It is easy to determine if an idea with a grand purpose is inert or not: simply observe employees. If they mouth the words but no one takes any action, the idea is inert. On the other hand, if everyone, from the forklift operator to the CEO, behaves congruently with the expressed purpose of the idea, it is not inert. For example, an SVP of a global construction company that valued the idea of Safety kept one hand on the railing as he walked up the stairs. As he did so, he mentioned to a passing senior manager coming down the stairs that he should do the same—because safety made the difference between the life and death of his employees. The idea of Safety was not inert in this company. Likewise, when Ray Kroc, the founder of McDonald's, was CEO, every restaurant manager knew that if he ever visited their location, he would stop to pick up any trash in the parking lot—because maintaining cleanliness was critical to the success of the business. It is said that he continued this behavior well after his retirement.

If an obviously important idea such as safety or cleanliness is not reflected in the everyday actions of people as they carry out their responsibilities, that idea is inert; and, this inertness will define the culture for all to see much more than all of the posters and brochures intended to promote the idea.

LONELY IDEAS

An idea becomes Lonely when no one wants to be near it, much less commit to it. Everyone may acknowledge that its purpose is worthy, and the required activities may be clear, but no one claims responsibility for its execution. In a meeting, when an idea is introduced with the words "Someone should . . ." you can expect that the idea will be a Lonely Idea. As everyone leaves the meeting without any individual specifically agreeing to be responsible for the idea, you know for sure it is a Lonely Idea.

Ironically, the phrase "We all should..." is equally likely to lead to an idea's abandonment. Heads may all nod as an immediate response to an idea introduced with this phrase, to indicate its acceptance by all. However, this almost ritual acknowledgement of the value of an idea may actually release group members from responsibility for individual action. Each individual in the room may say to himself, "If everyone has committed to take action, someone other than I certainly will." The idea becomes lonely in a crowd.

When a leader allows a meeting to end without someone being assigned responsibility to act on an idea that all have acknowledged as important, it usually means there is an unspoken agreement to avoid confronting the issues represented by the idea. This may be simply because it is an uncomfortable problem and no one wants to deal with it. Or there may be political reasons.

I once worked with an executive team whose meetings were consistently filled with discord that stemmed from conflicting egos and an inability to discuss differences in a rational manner. Everyone in the room knew that the problem existed. They each were aware that they were a dysfunctional team and that someone should do something about it. However, no one was willing to accept ownership of that idea and address the issue directly. Consequently, the unproductive meetings continued until the problem began to be noticed at higher levels.

This Lonely Idea of a Dysfunctional Team—the idea no one wanted to get close to—was finally addressed when I was brought in as an executive coach to help the group acknowledge the problem and develop some solutions. I didn't need to tell them there was a problem or that each had a role in the in it, because they all knew it. I only had to encourage them to accept ownership of the idea that they were a dysfunctional team so that each could accept responsibility for behaving differently. It is important to note that the entire executive team, and not only one or two individuals, had to take ownership of the idea of a Dysfunctional Team. This is because each had had a role in perpetuating the old way of doing things, and each needed to accept responsibility for new behaviors.

When you, as a leader, allow an idea to become ostracized so that no one is willing to talk about it, you make it a Lonely Idea. This may have an apparent short-term benefit of avoiding difficult issues, but the longer-term impact of developing a culture in which difficult issues can so easily be avoided can be significant. Likewise, when you and your people mouth ideas with important purposes but on which no one actually takes action—such as customer service, cleanliness, quality, or collaboration—you have allowed an idea to become lonely in a way that will undermine your credibility and that of your organization.

BUSY IDEAS

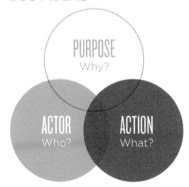

You have probably been entranced, in airports and museums, by entertaining contraptions in which rolling colored balls encounter levers, chutes, conveyor belts, elevators, pendulums, elastic bands and the like. The activity appears to have neither a beginning nor end and seemingly goes on forever. The fact that the thing has no obvious purpose does not keep us from becoming engaged. Such a machine is indeed busy as it uses complex devices to perform purposeless tasks in indirect, convoluted ways. This also describes employees engaged with Busy Ideas.

Busy Ideas are those that have no significant purpose but nevertheless require many people to take many actions without ever really knowing why. Some might refer to these actions as "busy work." Common explanations people give for taking actions without a purpose include "We've always done it this way" or "That's what I was told to do," or "It's in the procedure manual." Busy Ideas often reflect unquestioned but long-past valid assumptions or ingrained habits.

Busy Ideas are commonly born and reinforced when employees are paid for activity rather than impact. When this happens, the activity can become detached from its original purpose and develop into an end in itself. For example, a well-known drug store chain requires its counter staff to say to each customer, "Welcome to [company name], how are you today?" and their pay is reduced if mystery shoppers hired to check up on them find they forget to say it. The practice started a long time ago when customer surveys indicated the company stores were perceived as unfriendly. However, after years of repetition, the phrase has about as much meaning as, "Yeah, waddayuh want?" Nevertheless, employees continue to be rewarded for saying those words—and for perpetuating the now purposeless, but very busy, idea of a Customer-friendly Store.

The best way you can identify a Busy Idea within your organization is to wander through it, randomly asking people why they are doing what they are doing. If you don't get a clear answer, they may be trying to implement a Busy Idea—one requiring a lot of action that no longer has a purpose. Busy Ideas surrounding numbers sometimes leads to activities characterized as analysis paralysis. An organizational initiative that promotes new behaviors, without employees understanding or accepting their purpose, perpetuates Busy Ideas. Identifying these Busy Ideas allows a leader to reallocate resources to furthering ideas with more useful purposes.

IMMOBILIZED IDEAS

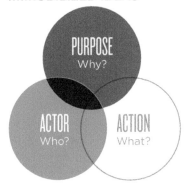

An idea without a clearly defined action is an idea with little possibility of impact. We all have lots of brilliant ideas immobilized within our heads—we want to invent something, start a business, write a book, take our career where it hasn't been before, build a house, go on a cruise, be what we want to be. The ideas are there for us to act on, but we seem unable to do so. It is not always a bad strategy to allow such ideas to remain immobilized because most people have more ideas than they have resources to carry them out. You simply can't do everything. However, almost everyone has at least several ideas they would really like to mobilize by taking action, but never do.

Fear is one reason people don't take action on ideas with purposes important to them. For example, someone wants to gain the skills of public speaking but is afraid to get in front of a group. Someone else wants to change careers, but is fearful of the economic risks. An executive wants to build a culture of caring but is afraid to introduce such a "soft" idea to his hard driving peers.

Uncertainty also causes immobility. People avoid acting on ideas important to them if they are uncertain about what would happen if they do so. They may also be stalled by uncertainty about what actions are appropriate for achieving their purpose.

Finally, confusion plays a role in immobilizing an idea—there are sometimes so many options available for action that individuals are unable to determine which is best and thus become paralyzed, taking no action at all. Many careers stall because individuals don't know how to sort through the confusion of too many options.

Your ideas need action plans if they are to have an impact. Some of these actions may be as simple as deciding to get up to get a cup of coffee. Others may need to be documented in complex process descriptions. You can't convert your idea into results if you haven't defined the required actions—it will become an Immobilized Idea.

Ideas delivered to an organization by corporate initiatives often arrive immobile. The activities of the initiative—getting a team together, creating promotional materials, putting on roll-out events—may be well articulated in a project plan and carried out as specified. However, the specific actions employees are to take to turn that idea into business results are often vague. As in the case of the Collaboration Initiative mentioned earlier in this chapter, a fine idea may be delivered to the organization, but employees will not accept delivery of the idea if they don't know what they are supposed to do with it, i.e., what actions they are to take to turn the idea into business results.

YOUR TURN

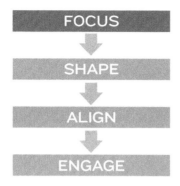

Step 1:
Focus Your Idea for Impact

This section guides you through a process of Focusing the Idea you identified at the beginning of the chapter. It includes:

DESCRIBE THE FOCUS OF YOUR IDEA.

CONDUCT A SUCCESS FACTOR ANALYSIS OF YOUR IDEA.

CONDUCT A RISK FACTOR ANALYSIS OF YOUR IDEA.

IDENTIFY SPECIFIC ACTIONS TO STRENGTHEN THE FOCUS OF YOUR IDEA.

Describe The Current Focus
Of Your Idea

WHAT ARE YOU THINKING?

Before you conduct your Success Factor and Risk Factor Analyses on the following pages, take a moment to describe the current focus of your idea.

The purpose of this step is to force you to think in extremely practical and concrete terms. Think about what you want to accomplish by delivering this idea to the organization and how people's behaviors will change as a result. Be as specific as possible on each entry and resist the temptation to add additional actors and actions. You can always do that later.

EXERCISE

Long-term purpose: Describe why is it important for the organization to adopt this idea.

Immediate objective: Describe what is expected as the immediate, measurable benefit if this idea is accepted and adopted by the organization.

Actors and actions: Identify three representative employees or stakeholders and indicate one specific action you will want each to take upon accepting this idea and integrating it into their work.

REPRESENTATIVE ACTOR	ACTION
PERSON #1:	
PERSON #2:	
PERSON #3:	

Success Factor Analysis: Focus

This and the following five pages describe five Success Factors related to the Focus of an idea. Having these five factors in place will significantly increase the likelihood that your idea will be delivered to the organization consistent with your original conception of it.

SUCCESS FACTORS RELATED TO FOCUS

1.1   Communication of the process and the idea

1.2   An idea rooted in reality

1.3   An involved and committed idea champion

1.4   Strong orientation to business outcomes

1.5   Clear and bi-directional accountability

The benefits of ensuring these Success Factors are in place include the following:

- Employees and other stakeholders will be more willing to accept the delivery of your idea because they will understand why the idea is important to the organization.
- People's actions will be more similar to what you hope for because they will have a clear idea of what those actions are.
- The immediate objectives and the long-term purpose of your idea will be more likely to be achieved. This is because employees and stakeholders will have a clear picture of the results you hope to achieve through their acceptance of your idea.

As you read about each of these Success Factors, think about how they apply to the idea you described on the previous page and how you might best accrue the above benefits.

COMMUNICATION OF THE PROCESS AND THE IDEA

As you plan and implement communications in the context of an initiative, it is important to distinguish between communications about the process (the initiative) used to move the idea forward, from communications about the idea itself. Each is important, but they serve different functions. Those charged with making the idea a success must remain aware of this difference or they are likely to focus on one to the exclusion of the other.

Communication about the process includes the what, when and how of a typical project, and its audience is the initiative team. Its primary function is to keep the initiative process on track as it moves the idea forward for delivery to the organization. On the other hand, communication about the idea being delivered relates to the status of the original idea as it is moved forward from conception to results. The audience for communication of the idea consists of the people in the organization who are expected to act on it once it is delivered. Most important, the communication about the idea continues after the idea is delivered to the organization. The function of communications about the idea is to ensure the original idea doesn't become lost in the shuffle of initiative activities and, especially, that it is accepted and adopted by those who must act on the idea over the long term.

It is relatively straightforward to standardize communications about the initiative process through update reports on tasks, schedules, resources expended and the like. On the other hand, communications about the idea being delivered by that process are more difficult because it is harder to discuss the status of an idea in concrete terms. This is why the idea of the Delightful Buying Experience in the earlier example ran into difficulties—while the software development process was closely monitored, the status of the critical idea of the customer experience was not. An emphasis on the process at the expense of the idea also happens when an idea is delivered through formal training. While program participant evaluations show the process of the classroom experience was enjoyable, no one evaluates the extent to which the idea presented in the program was accepted and implemented by the participants.

To what extent is this success factor in place?
    ☐ More than adequate
    ☐ Adequate
    ☐ Inadequate

AN IDEA ROOTED IN REALITY

For an idea to have an impact, it must be realistic from the beginning and remain realistic as a project or initiative moves it forward. Most important, it must be realistic when it is delivered to the people in the organization who must accept that delivery—which they will do only if they conclude that the purpose of the idea, and the activities required to achieve that purpose, are rooted in reality.

To ensure an idea is rooted in reality, aggressively challenge the assumptions you and others hold about the Focus of the idea: its Purpose, Actors and Actions. From day 1, challenge stakeholders—especially on-the-ground employees and their managers—to identify potential barriers that might impede the delivery of the idea to the organization or its acceptance by those expected to act on it. Prod them to think about a broad range of people who might create roadblocks to the idea, both during the initiative process and after the idea has been delivered to the organization. Ask also about formal and informal processes that might create bottlenecks, as well as intangibles such as attitudes, fears or perceptions that might inhibit people from accepting delivery of the idea and carrying it out.

Granted, it can be hard to ask for candid reactions to your idea and it may be harder for people to give them to you—especially if they see that you have already invested a lot in an initiative to promote it. But asking for a frank reality check from your employees and other stakeholders is the best alternative to burying your head in the sand. They may at first avoid giving honest answers but, if you ask the questions often enough—and listen to the answers non-defensively—they will begin to volunteer the information with the expectation that it will be well-received.

To what extent is this success factor in place?
    ☐ More than adequate
    ☐ Adequate
    ☐ Inadequate

AN INVOLVED AND COMMITTED IDEA CHAMPION

Most initiatives begin with an executive committed to an idea she has about a better organization. Because such a leader is very busy, she may not have taken sufficient time to think through the idea before handing it off to the team that will deliver it through the process of an initiative.

The term "hand off" must be correctly understood. Too many times it is taken to mean, "Give this idea to someone else to carry out so I don't have to think about it anymore." While it may be wise to hand off responsibility to the idea delivery process, a leader's commitment to the idea itself must be maintained. She needs to keep sufficiently in touch with the idea to ensure it is being handled correctly and doesn't get damaged in transit. She needs to be assured that, once the idea is delivered, it is the same idea she originally had in mind. Furthermore, she needs to make certain the organization knows, once the idea has been delivered to it, that it continues to be important to her.

The handoff of the idea from the leader to the initiative team is the time to ensure a clear and precise Focus of the idea: Its immediate and long-term Purpose and exactly who is supposed to do what in response to the idea, once it is delivered to the organization. It is also the time to confirm the relative importance of the idea, as compared to other ideas that could be handed off to other initiative teams for delivery to the organization's center stage. This will help the leader to determine if she has the personal and organizational resources required for her to champion the idea until it has been delivered to and fully integrated into the organization.

To what extent is this success factor in place?
- ☐ More than adequate
- ☐ Adequate
- ☐ Inadequate

STRONG ORIENTATION TO BUSINESS OUTCOMES

An organization is more likely to perceive the relevance of an idea if it is communicated as a set of business outcomes to be achieved rather than a set of actions to be carried out. A focus on business outcomes rather than activities will encourage individual initiative over blind obedience. This is not to downplay the importance of specifying actions when focusing an idea but, rather, of communicating those actions in terms of the ultimate purpose for which the idea is being delivered to the organization. Focusing employees' attention on business outcomes places the purpose of the idea directly in their field of vision.

When you use an initiative to deliver an idea to your organization, employees must understand exactly what they are expected to achieve by accepting and then acting on the idea. Then, they need the autonomy to achieve those business outcomes within the limits of risk, authority, flexibility and political realities that are acceptable to you. Holding people accountable for business outcomes rather than actions reduces complaints that "the folks in the executive suite are again asking us to do things we think are stupid." It also harnesses the creativity and intelligence of employees closest to the business—they may find ways to achieve the outcomes you desire more efficiently than the approach you initially envisioned.

To what extent is this success factor in place?   □ More than adequate

□ Adequate

□ Inadequate

CLEAR AND BI-DIRECTIONAL ACCOUNTABILITY

Every individual who is expected to act on the idea, and his direct supervisor, needs to know exactly what is expected of him. Delegate clear and specific responsibilities for each action required to achieve the purpose of the idea, as well as the results expected from those actions. These must be defined for each successive layer of the organization. Of course, this is easier said than done—but that can't be a reason for ignoring this obvious requirement. The key is to identify that set of actors, actions and results critical to your idea having the intended impact, to attach metrics to each component, and to prune out all but the essentials. The more you can narrow these down to the absolute minimum, the more practical it will be to create and monitor accountability.

The metrics by which each individual's performance will be measured must align well with the expectations of that individual's supervisor, the supervisor's manager, and up the chain of command. Then, managers and supervisors must be held accountable for communicating the message to their people, and for holding them accountable for their performance.

An important effect of this requirement is that all people involved in the idea will be forced to ask themselves, "So, what does this really mean in terms of day-to-day operations?" This, in turn, provides a reality check that holds a leader accountable for the wisdom of the idea and for providing the resources necessary to carry it out. This reality check is best done as the idea is being formed, or early in the initiative intended to carry it forward, rather than months—or even years—later when it may be discovered that no one knows exactly for what they are accountable at the ground level.

To what extent is this success factor in place?

- ☐ More than adequate
- ☐ Adequate
- ☐ Inadequate

Risk Factor Analysis: Focus

Any idea that you launch in your organization will face risks if you do not clearly define its Purpose, Actor(s) and their required Actions. This section presents the most common risks. Some of these I identified from my work with organizations and interviews with executives. Others are based on survey responses from my executive panel to the question "Why do initiatives fail?" The value of understanding these risk factors, and the indicators of their becoming a problem, is that you can spot problems more quickly and take steps to mitigate the risks.

RISK FACTORS RELATED TO FOCUS

1.1   The message doesn't get to the troops

1.2   The idea becomes disconnected from reality

1.3   Leadership loses interest

1.4   Actions become more important than results

1.5   Accountability disappears

Identifying and mitigating risks associated with an inadequately focused idea will help to avoid failures such as the following:

- An initiative generates a lot of energy that gets expended in so many directions that the net momentum is zero or even negative
- People generally acknowledge that the idea, and the initiative that moves it forward, are important—but no one takes any significant action to implement it.
- Employees and other stakeholders never quite understand why the idea is important or "what all the fuss is about."

As you read through these risk factors and, especially, the indicators of risk, think about which perhaps have already revealed themselves as potential problems and what steps you might take to mitigate these risks.

THE MESSAGE DOESN'T GET TO THE TROOPS

Inadequate communication is the number one risk faced by any initiative. While the nuts-and-bolts issues may be stated clearly in project plans, the idea behind the initiative tends to get short shrift—the product gets delivered but the idea has drifted away. This breakdown occurs for a variety of reasons. The most common is that the Focus of the idea—Purpose, Actor and Action—is not clear to those who initially conceived it and, thus, it can only be communicated unclearly. A lack of clarity about who is expected to take action once the idea is delivered to the organization is the most usual cause for this communication breakdown. This is because, if you don't know who is supposed to take action, you don't know who to talk to about making the idea happen.

RISK INDICATORS

- ☐ Those who are expected to change are unaware of that expectation.
- ☐ Employees cannot tell you who, what or why, when you ask about the idea behind the initiative.
- ☐ Ask ten employees about the idea promoted by an initiative and get ten different answers.
- ☐ You see that nothing changes at the ground level as a result of the idea.
- ☐ People don't ask questions about or comment on the idea during meetings, either during the initiative process or afterwards.
- ☐ The allocation of employee time or effort has not changed since the idea was delivered to the organization.

How important is this risk to your idea?

- ☐ Not important
- ☐ Important
- ☐ Critical

RISK MITIGATION: SEE SUCCESS FACTORS 1.1 & 1.5.

THE IDEA BECOMES DISCONNECTED FROM REALITY

An idea is disconnected from reality when it performs better in the minds of its creators than it does in the actual organizational environment. The most common source of this risk is that the executives who come up with the idea are also disconnected from reality. While these individuals may be aware of the financial status of the organization as well as other metrics of inputs, processes or outputs, they may be unaware of what employees do to achieve these numbers. Perhaps they have been out of the trenches too long or find themselves too busy to walk the floor. An idea thus created and then promoted through an initiative leaves employees scratching their heads and saying "huh?"

Ideas that are disconnected from reality are simply impractical. The sooner this disconnection is discovered, the better. Unfortunately, this basic risk factor is often not noticed until the initiative is well under way and the idea is already on the edge of failure.

RISK INDICATORS

- ☐ Leaders of an initiative can't describe the practical, ground-level impacts of the idea they are promoting.
- ☐ No one can explain what activities are going to be eliminated to allow for the idea to be carried out.
- ☐ The objectives to be achieved as a result of employees adopting the idea are too vague to be actionable.
- ☐ Time allocations and other resources are adequate to begin the initiative but not sustain the idea over the long term.

How important is this risk to your idea?

- ☐ Not important
- ☐ Important
- ☐ Critical

RISK MITIGATION: SEE SUCCESS FACTORS I.2 & I.4.

LEADERSHIP LOSES INTEREST

An organization's leaders lose interest in an idea because they lose track of its purpose. This can happen during the process of the initiative or after the idea has been delivered to the organization. They may have given insufficient consideration to the purpose during its creation, or it may have been intentionally kept ambiguous to avoid difficult discussions or tough decisions. When the beacon of purpose is lost, people will take whatever actions are most meaningful to them at the moment, and the impact of the idea will become lost. Often people, including the leaders themselves, are distracted from new ideas with new new ideas.

When the purpose of an idea is lost, it has become unimportant to leadership as well as employees. People no longer care. Perhaps it never was important to some, while others—even some who were considered "champions" of the idea—may have changed their mind or shifted priorities when they took a closer look.

RISK INDICATORS

- ☐ Updates on the status of an initiative, or the idea it is to promote, disappear from leadership reports, and no one asks for them.
- ☐ Direct reports of leaders can't give meaningful updates on the status of either the initiative or the idea it supports.
- ☐ Resources set aside for the promotion and implementation of the idea get allocated elsewhere.
- ☐ Activities required to carry out one idea conflict with those required by another idea promoted by yet another initiative.
- ☐ Organizational priorities shift, but no one tells the organization.

How important is this risk to your idea?　　　☐ Not important
　　　　　　　　　　　　　　　　　　　　　　☐ Important
　　　　　　　　　　　　　　　　　　　　　　☐ Critical

RISK MITIGATION: SEE SUCCESS FACTORS I.3 & I.5.

ACTIONS BECOME MORE IMPORTANT THAN RESULTS

Clarifying actions is an important part of focusing an idea. However, it is a bad sign if more focus is placed on the activities required by an idea than on the outcomes expected to result from people accepting it as their own. This sort of misplaced focus is always a risk because it is usually easier to measure and reward activities than results. When this happens, the idea may become what was described earlier as a "Busy Idea," with lots of activities and nothing to show for it.

One reason actions grab the center of attention while results are being ignored is that too many actions have been prescribed. Actions need to be pruned back to their essentials by asking the basic question: "Is this necessary to achieve the intended purpose of the idea?"

RISK INDICATORS

☐ Employees carry out activities required by an initiative, or to the idea it supports, but can't describe the relationship of these to business outcomes.

☐ Resources are expended in support of an idea, but there is no evidence of the connection between these expenditures and business outcomes.

☐ Documentation of the impact of the idea on the organization focuses on activities rather than results.

☐ Bonuses or other rewards are based on activities rather than on the results the activities are intended to achieve.

How important is this risk to your idea?

☐ Not important
☐ Important
☐ Critical

RISK MITIGATION: SEE SUCCESS FACTORS I.I, I.4 & I.5.

ACCOUNTABILITY DISAPPEARS

Lack of accountability for an idea is another way of saying that no one cares about it, no one feels responsible for it, and no one is personally committed to its success. Accountability is possible only when someone has specified who is expected to do what and by when. It also requires that those actors have each acknowledged their accountability. Most often, accountability is lost as the responsibility for the initiative process, and for the idea it is to deliver to the organization, is handed down the chain of command.

The reason accountability tends to disappear in successive downward hand-offs is that the Focus of the idea—its Purpose, Actors and Actions—have not been made sufficiently clear. Each handoff then adds additional ambiguity and opportunities for interpretation until the idea as originally conceived is no longer recognizable. Thus, momentum is lost at each handoff until, in the worse case, the delivery process is allowed to churn on until it dumps off an Inert, Busy, Immobile or Lonely Idea into the lap of the organization that won't have any interest in doing anything with it.

RISK INDICATORS

- ☐ There are no metrics for either progress or success in the implementation of the idea.
- ☐ Performance reviews do not reference progress of the idea or of the initiative that carries it forward.
- ☐ It is unclear to whom you can turn to obtain a definitive status report on the integration of the idea within the organization.
- ☐ Employees see no advantage in supporting the idea or participating in the initiative process.
- ☐ No one acknowledges responsibility for delays or missed objectives.

How important is this risk to your idea?

☐ Not important
☐ Important
☐ Critical

RISK MITIGATION: SEE SUCCESS FACTORS 1.3 & 1.5.

Thought-Provoking Questions
About The Focus Of Ideas

You will find that it is easier to think about the risks addressed in this chapter, and to help others think about them, by asking questions. To try this out yourself, ask yourself the following questions about one or more of the ideas you have considered in this chapter.

- How will this idea help us achieve our future vision? Strategic objectives? Mandate? Short-term objectives? [Purpose]

- How far down into the organization will this idea reach? Who will it affect? How will they know? [Actor]

- Exactly what will those affected have to do differently? Which new expectations will be most difficult for them? [Action]

- Who are other stakeholders of this idea? What actions will you need them to take? How will they know they need to take them? [Actor, Action]

- How do we know that achieving these short-and long-term purposes are worth the resources they will require? Why should we support this idea over other ideas? [Purpose]

NOW WHAT?

Review your assessment of the Success Factors and Risk Factors and indicate what actions, if any, are required to increase the effectiveness of your idea.

CHAPTER 2
Shape Your Idea For Understanding

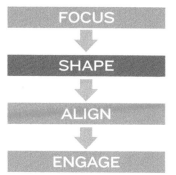

FOCUS

SHAPE

ALIGN

ENGAGE

STEP 2: SHAPE
IN A NUTSHELL

Your role as a leader is to anticipate the effect the shape of an idea will have on people's ability to pick it up, carry it with them or share it with others. This will increase the likelihood that it will have the impact you intend.

KEY POINTS

- The shape of an idea determines the efficiency with which it moves through the organization and varies on two dimensions:

    Simple-Complex: The number of components and relationships that are represented by your idea.

    Precise-Fuzzy: The degree to which your idea can be described in clear, exact terms.

- The interaction of these two dimensions create four basic shapes that influence how people understand and act on an idea:

    Pointed: Simple and precise, Pointed ideas provide extreme clarity of expectations but can also limit discretionary action.

    Cloudy: Simple and fuzzy, Cloudy ideas leave room for deliberation and negotiation, but can also forestall action.

    Turbulent: Complex and fuzzy, Turbulent ideas provide opportunities through new perspectives, but they can also create confusion, frustration and fear.

    Schematic: Complex and precise, Schematic ideas provide the detail essential to experts but can lead to confusion and rejection when forced upon non-experts.

BEFORE YOU START THIS CHAPTER:
PUT YOUR STAKE IN THE GROUND

The purpose of this very brief exercise is to encourage you to apply what you read in each chapter to a situation of your own. You may use the same idea you used for this purpose in Chapter 1, or you may want to identify another idea for this chapter.

EXERCISE

Describe how you refer to your idea:

_____

Give a short name or phrase you would use in normal conversation when discussing this idea. For example, it might be a single word, such as "Sales" or "competence" or a phrase such as "Bring product X to market in half the time we normally take."

Identify the 2-3 processes you will use or (have used / are using) to deliver this idea to the organization:

_____

_____

You may want to refer to this delivery process with a very broad term, such as "The New Product Rollout," but you will find it most useful if you can identify 2-3 more specific processes, such as:

- *"A series of monthly training programs taken by all mid-managers."*
- *"A national new-product meeting for all sales personnel."*
- *"Integration of new leadership competencies into annual performance reviews."*

IDEAS SHOULD BE PORTABLE

Imagine that your most important ideas are physical objects that can be picked up, manipulated or handed off. If you think of your ideas in this way, you will see that some are easier to handle than others. Some you can toss to a colleague, like a set of keys, and tell her to get in the driver's seat and take it down the road. Another may have a flat tire or two that needs to be repaired before it can begin to roll. Some look to be in fine shape on the outside but have serious defects under the hood.

This chapter will show you how to recognize the different shapes of ideas. Once you can differentiate ideas of different shapes, you will be able to anticipate the effect they will have on people's ability to pick up your ideas, carry them around and share them with others. When you understand how shape affects outcomes, you will be able to control what people do with your ideas more effectively and increase the likelihood that they will have the impact you intend.

An idea's shape is in two dimensions. The first dimension relates to the relative simplicity, versus complexity, of the idea. The second describes its relative precision, versus fuzziness. For an idea to have its desired impact, it must be shaped to meet the needs of the people who will handle the idea and the environment in which it must live. Sometimes ideas are inappropriately shaped from the time of their initial conception. Other times, the idea is suitably shaped initially but the process used to carry it forward—such as an initiative or project or even a meeting—damages it in ways that reduces its effectiveness.

Early in my career, I made a sales call on a mid-level management team at a prestigious Boston bank. We met in a plush conference room and each participant wore a well-tailored suit. Everything and every person in the room was neat and polished. Though I didn't realize it, these were important signs. The group was interested in a project management workshop I had under development. It was a pilot workshop, the formatting of the materials was not perfect, and there were some gaps in the content. Because of this, I presented the idea of The Project Management Workshop as a work-in-progress with opportunities for customization. They were not impressed and I didn't have another chance to make the sale. They were unhappy that my idea for a workshop was still a little rough around the edges. In retrospect, I should have anticipated this from the polished look of the place and people involved.

Later in the week, I used the same process to present my idea for a workshop to a group of project managers in the IT department of another financial services organization. We met in a conference room full of scribbled-on white boards and the dress was business casual. They became very engaged and asked me to submit a firm proposal. They were pleased, they said, that I hadn't offered them the typical slick presentation. Furthermore, they saw the gaps in content as an opportunity to insert their own ideas into the training program. They liked the fact that my idea of The Project Management Workshop still had some rough edges.

This and other experiences where "form" trumped "substance" have led me to conclude that the Shape of an idea affects its acceptance, and its longevity, at least as much as its content. It helped me to understand why some very good ideas fail to have an impact while some bad ideas manage to continue to live within an organization, seemingly forever.

The Shape of an idea has a direct impact on its success. Some people respond well to rough edges, some prefer them to be smooth. Some easily engage with soft and fuzzy ideas, perhaps colored with a bit of emotion. Others prefer ideas that are strictly fact-based and portrayed in precise black and white. Moreover, these relationships hold true whether we are talking about a strategic idea that is moved forward via the process of a large scale initiative, or lesser ideas that are carried forward by the process of a meeting or other day-to-day communication.

The fate of your idea depends, in part, on whether you shape it in a way that works for a given audience. As I learned when I made my presentation to the Boston bankers, the Shape of an idea is particularly critical when you have only one shot to present it for a decision, such as an initial sales call, a presentation to a potential investor, or a proposal to the board of directors. However, the Shape of an idea is also important as you shepherd it through the various stakeholder groups within your organization over an extended period of time.

The purpose of this chapter is to help you to think about the Shape of your idea and how that relates to what you want to accomplish with it. The appropriateness of a given shape depends on the idea's ultimate purpose as well as its stage in the process of an initiative, a project or a meeting that you use to move an idea from conception to business results.

THE FOUR BASIC SHAPES OF IDEAS

Ideas come in four basic shapes. You can identify these shapes by evaluating an idea's characteristics along two dimensions.

The **Precise-Fuzzy** dimension defines the degree to which you can describe your idea in clear, exact terms that everyone will understand in the same way as soon as they encounter it.

The **Simple-Complex** dimension describes the relative number of components and relationships that are represented by your idea.

These are not absolute dimensions but relative ones, i.e., they are most useful when comparing one idea to another, or the present state of your idea compared to a more useful state. For example, it is generally more practical to say "this idea needs to be more precise or more complex" than to try to specify exactly how precise or complex it is or needs to be.

The Shape diagram shows how the two dimensions interact to create the four basic shapes.

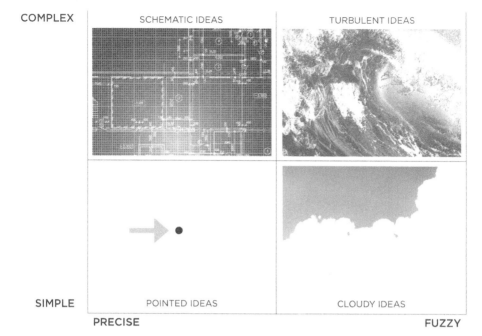

COMPLEX | SCHEMATIC IDEAS | TURBULENT IDEAS
SIMPLE | POINTED IDEAS | CLOUDY IDEAS
PRECISE | | FUZZY

Pointed ideas are both simple and precise. They are represented in the lower left-hand quadrant as a single, perfectly round dot. Extremely precise and simple ideas can often be represented as a single word or phrase that can lead to instant action. For example, the word "fire" shouted loudly and clearly represents the idea that "a danger is present and we need to get away from it now." When a sales rep says, "Sign here" or a customer says, "No," the words represent simple and precise ideas.

Cloudy ideas are simple and fuzzy and found in the lower-right quadrant. The motto, "A Great Place to Work!" at the top of a company newsletter is an example. So was the "Delightful Buying Experience" of the example mentioned in the introduction. Like the idea represented by "Fire!" this motto is also quite simple. However, unlike that idea, "A Great Place to Work!" is fairly fuzzy and could be interpreted quite differently by different people. You will find, later in this chapter, that a little fuzziness is not always a bad thing. However, any leader who wants to get serious about creating a "great place to work" needs to address the fuzzy quality of that idea, or risk having it mentally filed alongside "motherhood and apple pie."

Turbulent ideas are complex and fuzzy. In the upper-right quadrant, they are represented as a turbulent, stormy sea. Such a storm is complex because of the many interacting forces and the rate at which its many components change. It is fuzzy because those forces are not clearly understood by the average person. Moreover, there is often uncertainty about the storm's duration or the risk associated with being in the middle of it. Rumors of lay-offs or impending investigations usually are about Turbulent Ideas.

Schematic ideas are precise and complex and are found in the upper-left quadrant. These are represented by a blueprint, a document that has a large number of small, interrelated pieces defined in terms that any civil engineer would understand in exactly the same way. Ideas represented by detailed operational plans, legal documents, computer code or quantitative analyses share these characteristics. When experts and non-experts have difficulty communicating, it is often because the experts are most comfortable with the precise, complex form of the idea while the novice is easily overwhelmed by it.

For purposes of clarity, I have illustrated each quadrant with the most extreme example of its respective Shape. In reality, most ideas fall somewhere within these extremes. You will find that this simple framework will help you quickly categorize your ideas and those of others.

WORKING WITH IDEAS OF DIFFERENT SHAPES

Your job as a leader is to judge whether or not the Shape of your idea supports or hinders it from achieving its purpose, or if adjustments are required. It will be much easier to lead through ideas and improve the impact of your ideas when you are aware of their shapes and how to nudge them in the right direction and at the right time. In any organization, some people may see the same idea as having a very different shape than others do, depending on their perspectives, knowledge and experience. As a leader, therefore, you must understand how your ideas, and those of others, are perceived so you can determine risks to their success and intervene appropriately.

The Shape of an idea can provide some degree of insight about the level of risk it faces as it moves through the organization. I asked the Executive Panel to think about the initiatives they had seen fail over the previous ten years, and to indicate what shape ideas tended to have when they first perceived the idea was at risk of failing. The large majority of the group reported that ideas most often had a Tumultuous shape when they first appeared to be in trouble, followed by Cloudy, Schematic and Pointed shapes.

WHICH SHAPE IS AN IDEA MOST LIKELY TO HAVE WHEN YOU FIRST RECOGNIZE IT IS HEADED FOR AN EARLY DEMISE?

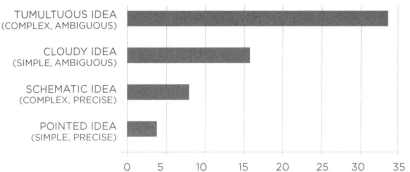

Pointed Ideas
[Simple, Precise]

Your idea is probably relatively simple and precise if you see that people immediately understand it and can communicate it to others with the same meaning you intend. If someone walks away with a confused look in his eyes or has to repeatedly ask for clarification, your idea is probably lacking the simplicity or precision appropriate to that individual.

ADVANTAGES OF POINTED IDEAS

People know exactly what you mean when you give them a Pointed Idea. If you tell someone what you want him to do, in simple and precise terms, he is likely to do it. This is very useful in emergency or crisis situations. It is also helpful when an idea has been tossed around or chewed on long enough that it is simply time to act.

Pointed Ideas are appropriate when many different people need to respond to them in exactly the same way, as when specific processes or procedures need to be followed for safety or legal reasons. Simple, precise ideas are necessary if you want everyone to follow exactly the same path.

Finally, Pointed Ideas work very well in chains of command where ideas need to be passed down the hierarchy and back up again. In these contexts, subordinates appreciate clear simplicity because it inspires their confidence and reduces the uncertainty of what is expected of them, and what the future will bring. Those higher in the chain appreciate people who can express their ideas in clear, crisp reports and recommendations. Military and other rapid-response organizations rely on Pointed Ideas, particularly in crisis situations or when teams from different organizational or national cultures are quickly formed to execute an idea. Hospital emergency personnel, first responders, and teams that respond to customer emergencies similarly rely on Pointed Ideas.

WHEN POINTED IDEAS ARE COUNTERPRODUCTIVE

Pointed Ideas leave employees little room for discretionary action. People may perceive them as intractable ideas that allow little opportunity for input and that minimize flexibility in execution. This can result in morale problems and may also prevent you from taking advantage of the insights and skills of your people. If you overuse Pointed Ideas, you may be perceived as dictatorial.

A number of years ago I was consulting with a retail store and happened to look into an employee break room. I saw dozens of little sticky notes of "do's and don'ts" posted on walls and bulletin boards to remind workers of everything from what to say to the customer under various circumstances, how to maintain the work area, how to check in and out, when and how forms must be submitted, etc. Many were faded or had curled edges, some were fairly new. Each probably got put up there as a legitimate solution to a problem observed by the store manager at one time in its history.

This was a great example of how, when there are so many of these little Pointed Ideas scattered about, they are simply ignored. (In some organizations, the equivalent of sticky notes on bulletin boards are policy and procedures manuals to which bullet points are added on a regular basis but only rarely culled out.) In addition, by posting a solution on a sticky note it became the only solution, thereby limiting the creativity of any employee who might have a better one. This is a great disadvantage of Pointed Ideas used in the wrong context. Pointed Ideas may also prevent you from taking advantage of the insights and skills of your people. To use this type of idea effectively as a leader, you must pay attention to when a Pointed Idea energizes employees, such as when you are leading the charge to a clear objective, and when it demoralizes them because they see no room for individual initiative.

Cloudy Ideas
[Simple, Fuzzy]

Simple, fuzzy ideas have indistinct edges which easily change in response to changes in the environment or when new information becomes available. Skilled sales reps are familiar with the value of Cloudy Ideas (although they don't call them that). They are generally useful at the beginning of the sales process, because they allow the exploration of possibilities with the customer before offering a specific solution. As a sales rep begins to understand the customer's needs, he can tighten up the idea as it moves forward in his sales process. Eventually, he develops it into a pointed solution tailored to the customer's problem. This is a balancing act because, if too much fuzziness is introduced into the initial discussion, the sales rep may be perceived as wasting the customer's time.

This demonstrates both the value and the risk of Cloudy Ideas: because of their intrinsic ambiguity, they are often interpreted through the lens of a viewer's unique insights—but also their personal biases.

ADVANTAGES OF CLOUDY IDEAS

Cloudy Ideas leave room for deliberation and negotiation. For example, the CEO of a major bank decided to change the culture of the organization to one of "customer focus." No one, including the CEO, knew exactly what this idea would mean in practical terms. What the senior executives knew for sure is, "we probably don't agree" on exactly how we need to change. What the CEO also knew was, if he would simply write a memo that would define it for everyone, his executives still wouldn't agree and would drag their feet because of it. This is why he introduced it in the form of a Cloudy Idea. One of those who I interviewed described the process that ensued as follows:

> "The idea [of customer focus] had a long gestation period...This was a good thing because senior managers had to articulate what they wanted and get in the same boat... It took people on top who were running the various businesses to come together and say, 'This is something that we jointly think is important."

This CEO exploited the fact that people feel some flexibility in their interpretation of a

Cloudy Idea, as compared to a Pointed Idea. For example, if you make the pointed statement "This is the way it is and this is what we are going to do about it," people may fall in line and do as they are told. On the other hand, if you say, "There are a number of ways of looking at this situation and I'd like to open the discussion of which makes the most sense," you will get a more varied response and will probably gain some new insights. Maintaining soft edges around an idea allows it to develop and mature in response to the input of a group. The leader in the case above recognized that, for this group, presenting an idea as a bit open-ended would promote collaborative discussion. He knew this because he knew the group. Other groups might prefer to approach the problem by having the leader describe one option in precise detail so they could each test it by arguing for their alternative. My message is to make your decision to use a Cloudy Idea consciously and with thought given to the nature of the group, not automatically use a Cloudy Idea any time you have a collaborative discussion.

In most circumstances, Cloudy Ideas are perceived with neutral or slightly positive emotions, because they pose no clear threat and people can interpret them as they wish. They may sometimes carry negative connotations, but not to the degree that they cause people to take action. For example, when employees sense a change is occurring in the organization but can't put their finger on what it is, they may become uneasy; but, since they don't have enough data to know whether or not they should be concerned, they are less likely to act on the simple, fuzzy idea of, "Something is going on around here..."

Pointed Ideas make it easier for people to dig in their heels whereas ideas with indistinct edges enable people to adjust their position without feeling like they have lost something in the process. Skilled negotiators know how to use fuzzy ideas to their advantage. If you start a negotiation by clearly stating exactly what you need for an acceptable result, the other side will do the same and the respective positions are likely to become entrenched. However, if you start the discussion around general issues and principles, you are able to sense what the person on the other side of the table feels about the issues at hand, and you will be able to craft options with which each of you are comfortable.

WHEN CLOUDY IDEAS ARE COUNTERPRODUCTIVE

Cloudy Ideas may be perceived as wishy-washy. If used in excess, they can lead people to wonder if you know what you are talking about or are willing to make a firm commitment.

Cloudy Ideas also don't move people to action, as Pointed Ideas do. When important aspects of an idea are unclear, such as the purpose of the idea, or its desired results, it is also unclear what to do in response to the idea. Cloudy Ideas tend to stall action because they don't communicate a sense of urgency.

For example, an R&D team for a medical equipment manufacturer felt they were hot on the trail of a breakthrough technology and were worried that a competitor would be first to market. They were sure their technology would have "therapeutic benefits," which was the basis for their ongoing corporate funding. However, they couldn't yet specify exactly what those "therapeutic benefits" would be. Therefore, they were unable to convince the board of directors to commit the resources necessary to bring the technology to market before the competition. The idea of Therapeutic Benefits was perceived as admirable, but did not have sufficient clarity or detail for the board of directors to accept the risk of allocating the resources necessary to put the project on a fast track.

In real life situations, a leader rarely faces extreme, either-or choices when presenting an idea. She doesn't have to choose a Pointed Idea or a Cloudy Idea. The fact is, either of these extreme options is likely to get a leader in trouble more often than not. In reality, the leader makes constant, more subtle adjustments to her ideas to shape them as the situation warrants. I will offer suggestions on how to monitor and maintain this tricky balance later in this chapter.

Turbulent Ideas
[Fuzzy, Complex]

 Turbulent Ideas are characterized by confusion and uncertainty. They make people uneasy because no one can tell if they are safe or not, and people don't know which way to turn for a more predictable future. For example, the following employee comments each represent a Turbulent Idea: "Things are going downhill fast and I don't know what anyone is doing about it," or "There are some big layoffs in the works, but I don't know where the ax will fall," or "I think the owners are trying to sell us to someone." These ideas have high levels of fuzziness and complexity as a result of an overload of conflicting and incomplete information. Almost everyone gets distracted by a looming unknown. Turbulent Ideas tend to result in lower productivity. They may even cause employees to leave for more comfortable environments.

For example, I worked with a software firm that was bought out by a much larger company. Since, by law, such transactions must be kept secret until they have been consummated, the purchase caught everyone by surprise. The idea of The Merger became turbulent because of the lack of information, and the complex set of possible next steps. People didn't even know if it was a merger or a takeover. While they knew there was going to be a reorganization, they had no idea what it would look like. They literally didn't know, each day, if they would have a job on the next day. To make things worse, it was going to be months before most of these details were to be worked out.

The impact of these Turbulent Ideas did have predictable consequences. Employee productivity declined significantly. More time was spent in discussions about the merger than in dealing with operational issues. People started looking for jobs and grabbed them when they found them, leaving holes in the organization's service line. By the time the details were finally worked out, the majority of key people had left and the remainder were sitting around, waiting to see what the future would bring them.

Other companies in similar situations limited the tumult, and its consequences, by creating a transition plan before the merger was announced. As soon as it was announced, employees were told in a large meeting, telecast throughout the organization, exactly what had happened and what the board's intentions were for the future. They were informed how personnel decisions would be made and the choices they would have available to them. While the news was not easy for many people, the disruption to ongoing work as well as the merger process was significantly lessened because the fuzzy complexity of the idea of The Merger was reduced.

ADVANTAGES OF TURBULENT IDEAS

Turbulent Ideas sometimes have positive effects. For example, less risk-averse people may be motivated to seek opportunities within the turbulence. At the same time, Turbulent Ideas can sometimes move employees to action—usually because people find them uncomfortable and would prefer to move to a more certain path, if you can show them one.

When people are averse to change or simply ignore the need for it, they may require encouragement. In this case, a leader sometimes presents the urgency for change by helping people to see the turbulence around them. In such a situation, they need to understand that if they don't do something different, the organization—and they themselves—will experience significant consequences. For example, a national retail chain recognized that its market share had been gradually sliding over the previous five years, and this was accompanied by a similar slide in customer satisfaction. Everyone in the organization was becoming quite anxious, from the executive suite down to the loading dock. In response, the company rolled out a nationwide event in which employees were first given some hard-hitting facts about the long-term consequences of these trends. This was immediately followed by very successful store-level planning sessions in which employees identified specific actions they could take to turn around this serious situation. This approach is sometimes described as calling attention to a "burning platform," in which the only rational response is to make change happen as quickly as possible.

Turbulent environments often provide opportunities for new and powerful ideas. This is partly because "necessity is the mother of invention." In fact, the joy of many entrepreneurs comes, in part, from the thrill of taking a chance on the edge of the unknown (just as artists, composers and modern dancers create new works only by working on the edge of what is accepted practice and what may be perceived by some as nonsensical). One of my clients, one of the nation's experts in pipeline safety who deals with extremely complex interactions of liquids and gases recently told me, "If I've done it before and I know exactly how to solve the problem, I don't find it very interesting." In addition, many of the most creative senior executives I have helped transition to new careers have told me that their first requirement for any new job is that they have to be able to delve into "messy problems." Turbulence loosens up the normal associations among ideas. It allows people to see old ideas from new perspectives and to discover new relationships among ideas. Risk-seeking problem-solvers crave the confusion created by Turbulent Ideas and love to dive into them to understand new possibilities.

WHEN TURBULENT IDEAS ARE COUNTERPRODUCTIVE

Turbulent Ideas function a bit like hurricanes. They are most likely to emerge when the emotional environment of the organization heats up, perhaps because of downward trends in the economy or unusual competitive threats. The environment grows increasingly turbulent. Additional bad news adds more fuzziness and complexity to the idea of "Something bad is happening to us!" So can rumors that circulate as people try to make sense of what's happening. Employees can begin to make decisions based on fear. Rumors grow well in such environments because they provide stories that allow people to temporarily make sense out of the confusion. Eventually, an unchecked turbulent system runs out of control, leaving leadership few options but to pick up the pieces after the storm.

Government leaders have concrete emergency plans for storms and, during hurricanes, information clearing centers prevent panic by providing real-time broadcasts of the storm status and emergency procedures. Likewise, effective business leaders have strategies to address turbulence. They calm the troubled waters by simplifying and clarifying people's perceptions of what is happening. They also dispel rumors by providing consistent, reliable information about exactly what is occurring and what to expect, both positive and negative. When you find yourself leading in turbulent times, the best approach is to share as much information as possible in the form of pointed ideas that address the present and future of the organizational chaos.

Schematic Ideas
[Complex, Precise]

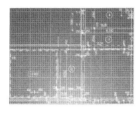

Schematic Ideas are both complex and precise, often with hierarchies of detail. Examples include blueprints, chemical processes defined by complex equations, the code supporting a software program, the esoteric rules, regulations and laws associated with a discipline, and other well-defined and integrated technical information. To the specialist, a Schematic Idea is no more than a collection of simple, precise ideas easily communicated to their colleagues. In the minds of non-experts, who don't understand the vocabulary or the profession's rules of communication, it may be as dense, confusing and threatening as a Turbulent Idea.

ADVANTAGES OF SCHEMATIC IDEAS

Schematic Ideas nail down everything that needs to be nailed down. The high level of detail allows experts to search out errors and contradictions. A software program can be debugged only when it has been written in absolute detail. A project to build a new plant cannot be well executed until every aspect of it has been planned and reviewed by technical experts in multiple disciplines.

Scientists and engineers are not alone in using Schematic Ideas. Accountants, financial analysts, lawyers, human resource professionals, and most other professions each have their own language with which to communicate ideas in precise, unfuzzy detail. In any specialty, it is impossible to develop complex systems without knowing the finest details of their components and how they relate to each other.

As a leader, you often do not have the expertise to evaluate the quality or completeness of most Schematic Ideas. This unusual characteristic of such ideas presents unique challenges.

WHEN SCHEMATIC IDEAS ARE COUNTERPRODUCTIVE

Experts may focus on the details, to the exclusion of the big picture; and, non-experts may be confused by the details to the extent that it becomes impossible for them to see their relevance to the big picture. Every professional has experienced mutual confusion when trying to communicate their expert insights to those who aren't schooled in their particular language.

When experts are asked to simplify their Schematic Ideas in a way that persons outside of their profession can understand them, they may feel they have to "dumb down" the ideas to the extent that they are no longer meaningful or valid. This tension is often observed in technical presentations to senior executives when, typically, the experts are given less time than they feel is required to provide all of the necessary details. In response, they create crowded PowerPoint slides with tiny text in an attempt to ensure their idea is delivered in full. A common reaction by the executives is to simply ignore the detail and view the entire slide as a black box. Frustrated executives, in this situation, may ask the equally frustrated experts, "Let's skip the analysis and cut to the chase," or simply plead, "Just give us a yes-or-no answer!"

Scientists and engineers experienced in dealing with senior executives know it is often best to simply leave out the detail, representing it literally as a "black box" that has clearly defined inputs and outputs but no hint about the details of its complicated interior. As a leader, you may understand the ingredients that go into a product or process along with the output that is sold to the customer. But, between the input and the output, you may have to depend on your experts to know what goes on in the black boxes.

This reality imposes certain obligations on you when you lead technology professionals. You need to know how to hire competent experts and how to communicate your business requirements to them so that they can take them into account in their analysis and recommendations. Then, you need to know how to evaluate the validity of their conclusions without entirely understanding how they came to them. In short, your ability to ask good questions and listen well to the answers, and your skill in assessing people, becomes more important than your expertise in a given profession.

YOUR TURN

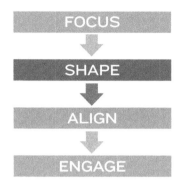

Step 2:
Shape Your Idea For Understanding

This section guides you through a process of Shaping the Idea you identified at the beginning of the chapter. It includes:

DESCRIBE THE SHAPE OF YOUR IDEA.

CONDUCT A SUCCESS FACTOR ANALYSIS OF YOUR IDEA.

CONDUCT A RISK FACTOR ANALYSIS OF YOUR IDEA.

IDENTIFY SPECIFIC ACTIONS TO IMPROVE THE SHAPE OF YOUR IDEA.

Describe The Current
Shape Of Your Idea

WHAT ARE YOU THINKING?

Before you conduct your Success Factor and Risk Factor Analyses on the following pages, take a moment to describe the current Shape of your idea from the perspective of others.

EXERCISE

a. Identify three representative employees or other stakeholders who you hope will take action on your idea.

b. For each person:

- Indicate the Shape of your idea as that individual currently sees it.

- Indicate, for that person, if the idea needs to be reshaped on the simple-complex or precise-fuzzy dimensions.

Helpful Hint: Remember that the names of the shapes and dimensions of precise-fuzzy and simple-complex are all relative terms—an idea may be fuzzy to one person and precise to another. It is more important to determine in which direction you need to nudge your idea than to decide in which quadrant it belongs.

REPRESENTATIVE EMPLOYEE OR OTHER STAKEHOLDER	SHAPE OF IDEA AS CURRENTLY PERCEIVED (Circle one)	HOW SHAPE SHOULD BE MODIFIED FOR THIS INDIVIDUAL (Circle one in each column)	
PERSON #1:	Pointed	More Precise	More Simple
	Cloudy	Keep as-is	Keep as-is
	Turbulent	More Fuzzy	More Complex
	Schematic		
PERSON #2:	Pointed	More Precise	More Simple
	Cloudy	Keep as-is	Keep as-is
	Turbulent	More Fuzzy	More Complex
	Schematic		
PERSON #3:	Pointed	Keep as-is	Keep as-is
	Cloudy	More Fuzzy	More Complex
	Turbulent		
	Schematic		

Success Factor Analysis: Shape

The following pages describe five Success Factors related to Shape that will increase the overall acceptance and impact of your idea. Having these Success Factors in place will help to ensure that your idea is shaped to fit the needs of those employees who you expect to pick up your idea, carry it around—perhaps enlisting the support of others—and then implement it.

SUCCESS FACTORS RELATED TO SHAPE

2.1 A 30-second elevator speech

2.2 Precise process and outcome metrics

2.3 Consistent vocabulary and framework

2.4 Systematic problem resolution

2.5 The idea remains in the spotlight

The benefits of attending to these Shape-related Success Factors include the following:

- Employees and other stakeholders will understand your idea at the detail that is required for them to act without confusing them with more than they need.

- As people hear about your idea and tell others about it, they are more likely to describe it accurately; and those they tell will also be more likely to repeat it accurately.

- Discussion about the idea and the initiative that carries it forward are more likely to be disciplined and efficient.

As you read about each of these Success Factors, think about how they apply to the idea you described on the previous page and how you might best accrue the above benefits.

A 30-SECOND ELEVATOR SPEECH

A short and succinct description of your idea is simply a requirement of effective branding, whether you are promoting the idea of a can of peas, the idea of what an engineering firm can do for its customers, or even the idea of you as a candidate for promotion. Most ideas that have gained significant momentum through the process of an organizational initiative are known by a simple name such as "Quality" or "Customer Satisfaction" or "Get it right the first time." This is because a simple name provides a conceptual handle that makes the idea easy to grab and hold on to. A 30-second elevator speech likewise provides a simple and precise picture of the idea—a picture that can be picked up and carried off by whoever comes in contact with it.

An idea that can't be clearly communicated in 30 seconds tends to become cloudier and cloudier as it drifts through the organization from one individual to another, until it is hardly visible. This is when people talk about it as having "faded into the woodwork."

A short and sweet version of an idea is particularly important for keeping secondary stakeholders in the loop. These include those who will be impacted by the idea or may eventually have to play a role in moving it forward, but who do not yet feel a personal involvement with it. They can inadvertently spread misinformation about the idea just because they don't understand it in simple and precise terms. The same people may later resist supporting the idea because they have already formed their own version of it that may indeed be simple and precise, but also inaccurate.

As in the case of any branding exercise, the message must be reiterated in multiple forms until it has created an indelible impression. This requires more than posters and slogans. It requires leaders to integrate the message into their conversations and presentations in a way that its relevance and practicality is obvious.

To what extent is this success factor in place?
☐ More than adequate
☐ Adequate
☐ Inadequate

PRECISE PROCESS AND OUTCOME METRICS

It is often said that you "get what you measure." One way this is true is that metrics provide a manager with benchmarks for rewarding or punishing desirable or undesirable performance. However, the more important benefit of clear metrics is that they clarify the idea that is being promoted. This benefit accrues as much to the leader who conceptualizes an idea as to those who implement it. For example, several leaders may agree that "collaboration" is a great idea but, until they are forced to define how they would measure it, they are likely to have very different ideas of what is meant by that term. (I saw this when I worked with the software company I described in chapter 1). I have frequently helped companies to develop assessment instruments to measure employee aptitude, attitude or performance. I have also developed measures of organizational characteristics such as quality, process efficiency, communication and the like. I have always felt the most important benefit of creating assessments is that it forces the leadership to clarify in their own minds what they mean when they discuss these sometimes fuzzy ideas.

Defining metrics when an idea is first conceived focuses pointed discussions on exactly what the idea is, where it is on its path to success and what needs to be done to keep it moving forward. It also clarifies the impacts expected to result from an idea. The level of precision required to identify process and outcome metrics forces clarity of thought and discussion about the idea itself. In this way, measurement tools can translate fuzzy excitement about an idea into focused energy with a higher probability of meaningful impact.

To what extent is this success factor in place?

- ☐ More than adequate
- ☐ Adequate
- ☐ Inadequate

CONSISTENT VOCABULARY AND FRAMEWORK

A clearly defined framework through which employees view an idea and a vocabulary with which to discuss it is necessary if they are expected to accept the idea, think about it, and integrate it into their work. This framework may take the form of a structured vision of the future, or a picture of the change in terms of "what is" vs. "what will be," or even a simple flow diagram or other graphic model. However, the specific form an idea assumes isn't as important as its consistency. A consistent framework and vocabulary imposes rationality on thought and discussion among employees as they encounter and interact with the idea. This allows less room for confusion.

Once you establish a vocabulary and framework for the idea you are promoting, you should organize meeting agendas around it, require participants' update reports to reflect it, and ensure that all communications and PR material use it. Don't allow alternative vocabularies to creep in and, if different words are used to describe the same thing, ask for clarification. When you observe that the initiative threatens to become fuzzy or confusing, step back and view it through the established framework. If the framework no longer works, refine it. If people are confused because they have lost track of the pieces of the idea or how they relate to each other, then reduce the complexity by reestablishing and reinforcing the common framework and vocabulary as simply and precisely as possible. Fuzziness and unnecessary complexity soak up energy. A clear framework and vocabulary focus that energy on achieving results.

To what extent is this success factor in place?

☐ More than adequate
☐ Adequate
☐ Inadequate

SYSTEMATIC PROBLEM RESOLUTION

The value of shaping an idea with simplicity and precision applies well to meetings convened to solve problems related to moving an idea forward. Traditionally, most such meeting agendas list issues to be discussed. For example, an agenda item might be "Friction between the R&D and Marketing groups." This approach can be counter-productive because it encourages general discussion with no clearly defined end. These discussions typically continue until the time allocated for the discussion runs out. On the other hand, listing agenda items as questions to be answered adds a greater level of simplicity and precision to the discussion and its purpose. For example, the same agenda item could be written as: "What is the central issue causing friction between the R&D and Marketing groups?" and "What specific steps can we take to resolve this issue?"

This simple practice of framing problem-solving discussions with questions to be answered, rather than issues to be discussed, creates a precise focus to the exercise. More important, it defines a precise end to the conversation—once the question is answered, the meeting can move on. If any part of the discussion wavers from that focus, you can table it and move back to the question. If a discussion seems to be chasing its tail, stop it and ask: "So, what question are we trying to answer, and what information do we need to answer it?" A systematic approach to identifying and solving problems adds to the precision of thought and communication that leads to the success of an idea.

To what extent is this success factor in place?

☐ More than adequate
☐ Adequate
☐ Inadequate

THE IDEA REMAINS IN THE SPOTLIGHT

If an idea is worth the expenditure of the time, energy and other resources required of a typical initiative, it is worth focusing the organization's attention on it. Keeping an idea in the spotlight allows its health to be monitored and its progress celebrated. It also may reveal flaws, even fatal ones indicating the plug should be pulled: the idea may no longer make logical sense, it may be inconsistent with organizational goals, or it may conflict with other initiatives also underway. Often the inclination of those responsible for a failing idea is to gradually dim the lights, so the flaws won't be noticed— or to allow it to slink off into the recesses of the organization. This is, in fact, a key reason why an idea that starts with a lot of hoopla ends up disappearing off the organization's radar while it continues soaking up valuable resources and decreasing leadership credibility.

Keeping important ideas in the spotlight also serves the purpose of clarifying to all exactly how many major ideas are vying for attention within the organization. Most organizations are "serial initiators," i.e., no sooner have they launched one initiative than they are off launching another. This leaves a very crowded stage with an audience wondering where it should focus its attention. When an organization is bombarded with one initiative after another, people learn to take cover each time a new one appears, saying to each other, "This too shall pass." Keeping ideas under the spotlight makes it evident when there are simply too many of them to succeed, so that someone can do some serious culling.

To what extent is this success factor in place?
      □ More than adequate
      □ Adequate
      □ Inadequate

Risk Factor Analysis: Shape

There is rarely a "right" or "wrong" Shape of an idea. Rather, an idea is shaped "right" or "wrong" for a given constituency.

RISK FACTORS RELATED TO SHAPE

2.1 A simply-stated idea is mistaken for a simple idea

2.2 Feeling good is the primary outcome

2.3 The idea becomes mired in complexity

2.4 Momentum is yielded to analysis paralysis

2.5 The initiative fades into the woodwork

Identifying and mitigating risks associated with an idea having an inappropriate shape for a given constituency will help you avoid problems such as the following:

- Experts involved with developing the initiative process have difficulty communicating with non-experts who don't have a firm grasp of the underlying principles that support the idea.
- The conceptual framework and vocabulary used to discuss the initiative, and the idea it supports, are so inconsistent across constituents that coordination and collaboration becomes difficult.
- People are unable to accept delivery of the idea simply because they can't get clear on what it represents or what they should do with it.

As you review the following risk factors, and the related risk indicators, think about ways in which you might juggle the characteristics of simplicity vs. complexity and precision vs. fuzziness to meet the needs of those people who you wish to accept and act on your idea.

A SIMPLY-STATED IDEA IS MISTAKEN FOR A SIMPLE IDEA

The same simplicity that can sell an idea can derail it when team members, employees and other stakeholders believe that the idea is as simple as the elevator speech—and they allocate their time, attention and other resources accordingly.

The challenge to a leader is to maintain the balance of simplicity and complexity of the idea being delivered to the organization, and to modify it according to the audience. It may be useful to think of a simple-precise message as a package that contains increasing levels of complexity as it is opened and the contents are put to use. The important thing is that, while people may be initially attracted by the simplicity of the package, they are not surprised or disappointed as they open it and begin to understand its deeper complexity—and the demands it will place on the individuals and the organization.

RISK INDICATORS

- ☐ An idea doesn't move beyond slogans and posters.
- ☐ More resources are put into publicity than implementation.
- ☐ Proponents of the idea cannot describe details of implementation of the initiative or the impact of the idea on the organization.
- ☐ Responsibility for an initiative is handed off to subordinates with only a bare-bones description that provides little direction.
- ☐ People expected to take action once the idea is delivered to them can give only superficial explanations of what it is about.

How important is this risk to your idea?

☐ Not important
☐ Important
☐ Critical

RISK MITIGATION: SEE SUCCESS FACTORS 2.1 & 2.2.

FEELING GOOD IS THE PRIMARY OUTCOME

Enthusiasm is usually a good thing. It becomes a bad thing when it is taken as the primary indicator of success. For example, an employee health initiative became very popular during its twelve-month roll-out as employees took exercise breaks and were given discounts to exercise facilities. The idea was that the availability of such activities would yield healthier employees.

The initiative was a personally rewarding experience for the initiative team members as well as employees. When the idea was rolled out to the entire organization, team members and sponsoring executives celebrated their success at the initiative completion party.

Unfortunately, there was no way anyone could determine if the idea achieved its purpose or not, since health-related metrics were never followed up. I have witnessed enthusiastic celebrations for initiatives that later proved to be dismal failures. However, the failures were never noticed because the fuzzy qualities of feeling good distracted attention from the need for specific and precise evidence of impact.

RISK INDICATORS

- ☐ Announcements of good intentions satisfy the desire for change.
- ☐ General goals don't evolve to specific plans.
- ☐ Employees get enthused about the idea as it is rolled out, even though there is no specific plan for follow-through.
- ☐ Leaders congratulate themselves on a job well done after an outstanding kick-off meeting but before the idea has had any impact.
- ☐ Team members believe their own promotional materials with no evidence the promised benefits were achieved.

How important is this risk to your idea?
☐ Not important
☐ Important
☐ Critical

RISK MITIGATION: SEE SUCCESS FACTOR 2.2.

THE IDEA BECOMES MIRED IN COMPLEXITY

If "too many cooks spoil the broth," this is especially true when each comes with his own recipe and doesn't share it with the others. While successful initiatives require broad collaboration, many fail because they were created by a committee that was never quite able to collaborate, providing the basis for another common quip, "A camel is a horse created by a committee."

The cause of this confusion is usually that stakeholders never achieved clarity on what they were trying to accomplish or how they were trying to accomplish it. As different advocates move forward on different assumptions on everything from purpose to desired outcomes of the idea, the idea increases in both complexity and fuzziness—it becomes turbulent. The consequence of this confusion is that it takes too much time to get the idea launched and, once it is, the idea fails because of its ineffective shape.

RISK INDICATORS

- [ ] The same issues are discussed repeatedly without resolution.
- [ ] Members of the same team provide conflicting updates.
- [ ] Status reports are inconsistent in format and lack details.
- [ ] Team members and stakeholders resist efforts to get specific on the idea or the progress toward its acceptance and adoption by the organization.
- [ ] Issues are resolved through political power rather than intelligent discussion.

How important is this risk to your idea?
- [ ] Not important
- [ ] Important
- [ ] Critical

RISK MITIGATION: SEE SUCCESS FACTORS 2.1, 2.2. & 2.3.

MOMENTUM IS YIELDED TO ANALYSIS PARALYSIS

Some initiatives fail because unnecessarily extensive planning burns resources and depletes the momentum of the idea it is to deliver to the organization. This elaborate planning tends to focus primarily on the logistics of the initiative process at increasing levels of complexity and precision. However, it often neglects risk factors related to the less well-defined aspects of delivering an idea to the organization such as preparing the organization for change or developing the commitment or stakeholders. The result is an overly designed, unnecessarily complex creation that does not fit the needs of stakeholders or the environment in which the initiative is expected to thrive.

RISK INDICATORS

☐ Initiative components proliferate with limited communication among those responsible for them.

☐ More and more data is collected and analyzed while fewer and fewer decisions are made.

☐ Initiative meetings process endless details with little forward movement.

☐ More thought and discussion is devoted to designing and developing the initiative than to planning for its integration into the organization.

How important is this risk to your idea?

☐ Not important
☐ Important
☐ Critical

RISK MITIGATION: SEE SUCCESS FACTORS 2.1 & 2.4.

THE INITIATIVE FADES INTO THE WOODWORK

Never allow an initiative to slink off into the recesses of the organization where it can die a slow death of starvation. It is always better to kill it with a clear and precise blow than allow it to slowly fade away. Don't cave in to those who would prefer that the initiative simply disappear through benign neglect—insert it into the agenda when it is left off, and ask people to update the group on previous commitments. Call the question, "Is this still an active initiative to which we are giving our support, or not?" When this question results in awkward silence, pursue it to identify what the underlying issues are, and ask what needs to be done to resolve them. If the honest conclusion is, "Nope—we no longer believe this is an idea worth pursuing," then define a clear and precise plan to formally end the initiative. For the sake of the credibility of your next initiative, make sure this plan includes communications to employees and other stakeholders. Recognize their contributions and explain why the decision was made and exactly what steps need to be taken to close it down.

RISK INDICATORS

- ☐ Updates on the progress of an initiative disappear from executive reports.
- ☐ Key initiative team members gradually move to other projects.
- ☐ Timelines get extended and no one pays attention to them.
- ☐ Budgetary resources disappear or don't get renewed.
- ☐ The idea is no longer a topic of conversation.

How important is this risk to your idea?

- ☐ Not important
- ☐ Important
- ☐ Critical

RISK MITIGATION: SEE SUCCESS FACTORS 2.2., 2.3 & 2.5.

Thought-Provoking Questions
About The Shape Of Ideas

You will find that it is easier to think about the risks addressed in this chapter, and to help others think about them, by asking questions. To try this out yourself, ask yourself the following questions about one or more of the ideas you have considered in this chapter.

- What three phrases can you use to describe this idea or initiative in a way that all of your stakeholders will know exactly what it is about? [Pointed Ideas]

- Is this a warm and fuzzy idea? If so, exactly what do stakeholders expect will be different as a result of it? What different interpretations do people give to it when they first hear of it? Which of these interpretations conflict with each other? How will you bring clarity? [Cloudy Ideas]

- Who will find this idea scary, worrisome or frustrating because they are confused by it? How can you clarify their confusion or otherwise relieve their anxieties? [Turbulent Ideas]

- What details need to be worked out? What can go wrong with this idea, and what will you do to prevent it? What experts do you need to validate this idea? What details are unclear, and what do you need to do about that? [Schematic Ideas]

NOW WHAT?

Review your assessment of the Success Factors and Risk Factors and indicate what actions, if any, are required to increase the effectiveness of your idea.

CHAPTER 3
Align Your Idea For Synergy

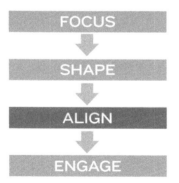

FOCUS

SHAPE

ALIGN

ENGAGE

STEP 3: ALIGNMENT
IN A NUTSHELL

Your role as a leader is to ensure the due diligence is conducted to identify aligned and misaligned ideas as you decide to initiate or continue an investment in an idea.

KEY POINTS

- Aligning an idea with existing strongly held ideas will result in more cost-efficient implementation because it can take advantage of the momentum of those ideas.

- Alignment of ideas within an organization is increased when a clear Future Vision provides a beacon to which those ideas can align. Those who develop ideas need to keep an eye on that beacon.

- Identifying misaligned ideas allows you to mitigate the related risks including being blind-sided, or blind-siding someone else.

- Developing alignment on each of four facets of an idea will take advantage of the momentum of related ideas.

  Objectives: Ideas that support the same outcomes and Future Vision will minimize wasted resources caused by their pulling against each other.

  Vocabulary: Ensuring everyone is using the same words to describe similar ideas decreases the risk of left hands not knowing what right hands are doing.

  Culture: An idea may work in one setting and yet be ineffective in another because some of its characteristics don't easily transfer across organizational or geographic boundaries.

  Structure: Redundancies and clashes of ideas can result when they are structured around different mental models based on everything from building layout to professional backgrounds.

PUT YOUR STAKE IN THE GROUND

The purpose of this very brief exercise is to encourage you to apply what you read in each chapter to a situation of your own. You may use the same idea you used for this purpose in one of the previous chapters, or you may want to identify another idea for this chapter.

EXERCISE

Describe how you refer to your idea:

_____

Give a short name or phrase you would use in normal conversation when discussing this idea. For example, it might be a single word, such as "Quality" or "Satisfaction," or a phrase such as "Increase revenue through enterprise sales."

Identify the 2-3 processes you will use or (have used / are using) to deliver this idea to the organization:

_____

_____

You may want to refer to this delivery process with a very broad term, such as "The Collaboration Initiative," but you will find it most useful if you can identify 2-3 more specific processes, such as:

- *"An on-line simulation of collaboration challenges for engineers."*
- *"Develop a database of collaboration best practices."*
- *"A blog authored by the Chief Technology Officer on the issue of collaboration."*

THE VALUE OF ALIGNMENT

Ideas are aligned when they result in individuals and teams pulling in the same direction in support of a common mission. Misaligned ideas are evident when individuals and teams work at cross purposes to each other or fail to exploit opportunities for synergy.

Aligned Ideas have a greater chance of survival than those that travel through an organization independently of each other. Likewise, Aligned Ideas are better able to achieve the synergy of shared financial, intellectual and political resources. The degree to which your ideas align with the ideas of others will determine the level of collaboration you can build and the amount of resources you will have to spend to achieve the impact you desire.

Ensuring your idea is making the most of its alignment with others should be part of the due diligence process you go through as you decide whether it is the right idea for the right time. This involves digging around a bit to find out what ideas are out there that could give yours a lift or perhaps act as a barrier. You will want to assess the extent to which they are aligned with your idea and your organization's Future Vision. Then, as you identify these ideas, you need to assess their alignment in terms of four different facets: Objectives, Vocabulary, Culture and Structure.

Sources Of Misalignment— Understanding The Environment For Your Idea

You cannot understand the degree of Alignment of your ideas with those of others if you aren't in close touch with the environment in which you expect your idea to flourish. You need to be aware not only of what other ideas are being advanced but also what processes are being used to advance them. Sometimes these are hidden from view because those responsible for them haven't thought of the importance of collaborating with those who might have similar ideas.

Sometimes the process used to move an idea through the organization, from conception to results, encapsulates or insulates the idea from the rest of the organization so that alignment with other ideas in the organization becomes very difficult. When this happens, the team may miss opportunities to take advantage of the momentum of other ideas headed in the same direction. For example, a team within a manufacturing plant in the Eastern US was responsible for a local initiative to inculcate the idea of Getting it Right the First Time into all areas of the plant. Because this idea was conceived by the respected plant manager, the team approached that process enthusiastically with a "heads down, full speed ahead" attitude. Their intention was to create a model that, while developed locally, could be used by its several sister plants scattered over the country. However, because team members had such a heads-down focus on making this project a success, they never put their heads up to notice that a similar idea was already being carried forward by a similar project in a plant in the Western US. Because the Eastern project team remained unaware of this parallel effort in the Western plant, they were unable to take advantage of the synergy that could have resulted from collaboration. This is an example in which focusing on the local process designed to move an idea forward and "get it out the door" actually insulated the idea from the rest of the organization—limiting synergy through alignment and lessening the overall impact of the idea.

Misalignment can also occur when multiple processes are used to move forward similar ideas within the same organization, working at cross purposes so they actually yield conflicting results. Several decades ago I developed customer and sales support materials for the rapidly expanding line of fax machines of a major office equipment manufacturer. Their machines' ease of use was thought to provide an important competitive advantage in achieving the organization's goal of customer satisfaction. Thus, the idea of Ease of Use was promoted at all levels of the organization. For example, both the product design group and the sales organization independently promoted the idea within their organizations through a variety of processes including training programs, lunch-and-learns and other forms of internal communications. But, I was frequently struck by the differences in how the product design engineers and the sales personnel viewed and implemented the idea of Ease of Use: The engineers took it to mean that a fax machine's menu should be structured in an extremely logical and hierarchical tree format—just like they structured its circuitry during the design process. They felt this logical organization would make their products easy to use and, thus, would lead to increased customer satisfaction.

Those in the sales organization, on the other hand, understood the idea of Ease of Use from a different perspective. They interpreted it to mean that the menu items would be organized around the tasks customers performed most frequently, in the order in which they performed them. This disconnect between the two conceptions of the idea of Ease of Use was due to a lack of collaboration between the two groups responsible for the carrying the idea forward within the organization. This resulted in frustrated engineers and sales reps as well as confused and dissatisfied customers.

This is a common disconnect within organizations: technical experts organize information about an idea according to how professionals in their discipline think rather than how laypersons think. The underlying idea may be the same, but the two groups sometimes have difficulty collaborating because the ways in which they think about their ideas don't align. In the case of the fax machines, this misalignment impeded progress toward a common vision of customer satisfaction.

THE ROLE OF A FUTURE VISION

The most important thing you can do to ensure alignment of ideas within your organization is to have a clearly articulated Future Vision that can serve as an orienting beacon. As a leader, you want all ideas within your organization to be aligned with that vision, including the short-term Immediate Ideas, the mid-term Tactical Ideas and the long-term Strategic Ideas. Unfortunately, this ideal is far from the reality in any organization.

If you, as your organization's leader, do not clearly articulate your idea of the future, perhaps because you don't have it well defined in your own mind, leaders of smaller business units will each create their own. When your Future Vision is unclear, the likelihood that other ideas within your organization are aligned is very low.

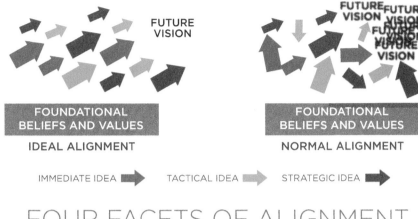

FOUR FACETS OF ALIGNMENT AMONG IDEAS

Alignment of the various ideas within an organization with its Future Vision is essential. But the degree to which those ideas are aligned with each other is also critical to maximizing the momentum of individual ideas—as well as the net momentum of multiple related ideas. As you conduct your due diligence before initiating a process to move an idea forward through the organization, it may save you time, money and perhaps political strife, to do an internal search for other active ideas that might help or hinder yours. People may refer to the processes that move these ideas forward as initiatives, but they might also call them activities, projects, reorganizations, upgrades, etc. This variety of nomenclature may provide a challenge to your due diligence because it may disguise the fact that others are trying to promote ideas similar to yours to accomplish similar goals.

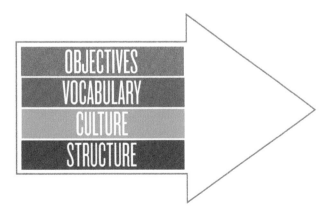

Ideas can be aligned with each other in terms of four different facets. The more your idea is different from another idea on any of these facets, the less they are aligned, and the less likely it is that they can build on each other's momentum. Severe misalignment on any of these facets can result in the two ideas working against each other.

To understand the relative importance of each of these facets, I asked the Executive Review Group to again reflect on the failed initiatives with which they were familiar and to estimate how often each of these factors played a role in those failures. Their responses indicate that the misalignment of objectives and cultures played a role most frequently, followed by the misalignment of structures and vocabularies.

The examples that follow provide perspectives on how the misalignment of ideas on each of these facets occurs, the consequences that result, and what you can do to harness the momentum of other ideas to your own to achieve a greater impact with fewer resources.

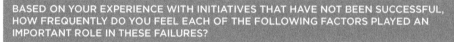

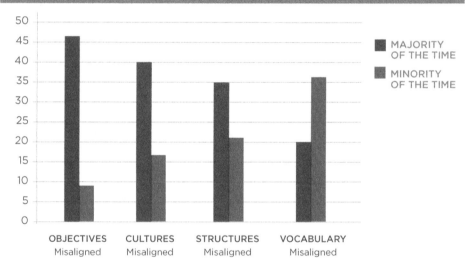

ALIGNMENT OF OBJECTIVES

The Objectives of two ideas are aligned with each other if they support similar outcomes as well as the same Future Vision. If the Objectives are complementary, i.e., they are additive, the two ideas will profit from the other's forward progress. However, to the extent that Objectives are duplicative, and the overlap is not recognized, resources are likely to be wasted as the closely-related ideas are pursued.

When the Objectives of two ideas are not aligned, the best case scenario is that the ideas don't get in each other's way. At worst, they can waste resources and cancel out any positive effect the other might have. The example in the shaded box describes a bank that attempted to move forward two ideas that worked against each other because they had misaligned Objectives. Each idea was promoted through a different process: the first through a marketing initiative and the other through a sales initiative.

MISALIGNED OBJECTIVES OF TWO INITIATIVES

BACKGROUND:
The CEO of a bank serving rural communities designs a clear Future Vision: To hold a 40% market share of high value customers within target communities within four years. Two initiatives have been launched, one by the marketing department and the other by the VP for sales.

IDEA #1:
Build close relationships with high value customers who are well-established in the community.

THE PROCESS:
A marketing initiative named "Make it Personal!"

OBJECTIVE:
Develop deep, trusting relationships within customer communities so that high-value customers will turn to us first.

ACTORS/ACTIONS:
Local bank executives will spend personal time with their community's business leaders, participating in community events, joining the boards of non-profit organizations and the like.

IDEA #2:
Motivate employees to acquire new customers with high value potential.

THE PROCESS:
A sales initiative named "Results Based Compensation"

OBJECTIVE:
Acquire as many potential high value customers as possible from our competitors and from the new resident population.

ACTORS/ACTIONS:
Local bank executives and their staff will cold-call prospective customers with high value demographics to sign them up. Bonuses will be awarded on increases in numbers of customers and quarterly contests will reward exceptional results.

THE IMPACT OF THE MISALIGNED OBJECTIVES:
The marketing and the sales initiatives may each promote a good idea, each of which are aligned with the CEO's Future Vision of a 40% market share of high value customers in four years. However, the ideas are at cross-purposes with each other: on one hand, the idea promoted by the "Make it Personal" initiative, a process requiring quality time to be spent with potential high value customers, has the objective of developing deep relationships; on the other hand, the idea promoted by the "Results-Based Compensation" initiative, a process that rewards relatively superficial relationships, has the objective of signing up the maximum number of potential high value customers. As a result, employees and their

managers became confused and demoralized as the ideas supported by the "Results-Based Compensation" initiative and the "Make it Personal!" initiative subverted each other.

This example of misaligned objectives illustrates the importance of looking around, when you plan to move an idea forward within your organization, so you can find opportunities to collaborate with others and avoid conflicts as well as duplication of effort. Once you start thinking in these terms, you will find that this advice applies as well to ideas that are on a smaller scale than those associated with the typical corporate initiative. For example, have you ever observed a two-person sales call or presentation when a sales associate had the objective of persuading the customer to sign on the dotted line, while the technical support person saw his objective as explaining the fine points of how the product works? Or, how about the idea of an Annual Performance Review? The manager may see the objective of this idea as providing constructive feedback, while the employee is there with the primary objective of finding out if he is getting a raise. When the objectives of two similar ideas are at odds with each other, one or both will not achieve its desired impact.

Your idea is more likely to have the impact you desire if you have clear in your own mind the objectives you are trying to achieve, and if you share your objectives with others who may be affected by it. This is particularly true if you are collaborating with others and want to avoid a tug-of-war for time, money or political support.

ALIGNMENT OF VOCABULARY

Alignment of Vocabulary simply means that all parties involved with a particular idea use the same language and mean the same thing when they communicate. As obvious as this may seem, the lack of a common Vocabulary for related ideas within an organization often leads to wasted resources because confusion and miscommunication create a situation where left hands don't know what right hands are doing.

For example, every professional discipline uses some sort of problem-solving process that begins with collecting information and defining the problem, and ends with creating and testing a solution. However, the various professions use different words to define each phase. Software developers may call the first step of their problem-solving process a 'requirements analysis.' Engineers in the same company might call their first step a 'design definition.' When architects begin their work, they may call it 'programming.' When instructional designers scope out a training design they may call it 'needs assessment.' Financial modelers may refer to the first phase of their problem-solving process as 'specification identification.' Subsequent phases of the problem solving process used by these various professions likewise may be called different names by each of them. The fact that these processes are a lot more alike than they are different is often masked by this terminology, creating a barrier to understanding and collaboration with people outside of the profession. It is amusing to watch the interactions of two such groups, such as when software developers meet with instructional designers for the first time, and note how long it takes before the lights start going off in their respective brains and one or the other announces, "Oh, I get it. We're both talking about the same thing!"

Misalignment also occurs when two parties use the same terminology to refer to different ideas, leading them to believe their ideas are aligned when they are not. As the following example illustrates, this can cause as much confusion as using different words to describe the same idea.

MISALIGNED VOCABULARY IN A MERGER

BACKGROUND:
Two major banks merged, and senior executives from similar functions in each organization sat down to compare policies and procedures to identify potential conflicts. The conversation focused on the management level at which structured finance deals could be approved. Both groups assumed they were talking about the same thing.

WHAT THEY CALLED THE IDEA: "Structured Finance Deals"

THE MISALIGNMENT:
Although participants left the meeting believing that both organizations approved structured finance deals of a certain value at the Senior Vice President level, they later found out that this wasn't at all true because they each had a very different idea about what that phrase "structured finance deals" meant. The problem emerged not from people using different words for the same thing, but by using the same words for different things.

THE IMPACT OF THE MISALIGNMENT:
Team members didn't realize the problem until procedures related to structured finance deals were designed into job descriptions, process maps and software. This resulted in costly rework that put the team behind schedule and, in the meantime, led to a lot of dysfunctional finger pointing. A bit of time spent up front to define terms would have avoided the difficulty.

I interviewed one of the participants in this meeting, who reported:

> We were literally using two different languages, but we didn't know it because we were using exactly the same words. But not until you looked at the detail side-by-side did you see that one group's deals were significantly further down the complexity and riskiness chain than the others were. In a merger, you need to continue to ask yourself, "Are we talking about the same thing?"

When cross-functional, inter-divisional or even international teams work together in an organization in which the vocabulary for ideas is aligned, only a minimum amount of time is required to establish a working relationship. They sit down and get to work as if they have collaborated all of their lives. When a consistent vocabulary does not exist, most language problems do eventually rectify themselves once people from different backgrounds have worked together for a time. However, the confusion sowed in the process can be substantial. Your role as a leader is to minimize the confusion by encouraging common vocabularies for ideas that transcend departments or disciplines. This helps you to nurture a silo-free culture that seeks out and capitalizes on similarities while also leveraging legitimate differences in perspectives and ideas.

ALIGNMENT OF CULTURES

An idea may work in one setting and yet be ineffective in another because some of its characteristics don't easily transfer across cultural boundaries. The idea may also be viewed differently from one culture to another. While this is easiest to imagine between national cultures, similar problems happen between different corporate cultures, business unit cultures and even team cultures.

For example, engineering or other scientific groups often create cultures that value precisely communicated ideas, unfuzzy definitions of terms, clearly stated assumptions, and logical arguments. On the other hand, sales organizations are much more tolerant of flexible terminology adjusted to fit the perspectives of a particular customer. They may be as interested in how their customers feel about the ideas they present as they are in how they think about them. This is the reason sales people often prefer that a technical expert not participate in a sales call and why many engineers would just as soon not have sales or marketing staff participate in their product development discussions.

Cultural differences such as these can create silos within organizations and invisible barriers between groups. These obstacles are usually not acknowledged because they are felt more than seen. Consequently, the lack of Alignment may manifest itself in dysfunctional relationships between headquarters and field organizations, line and staff functions, parent companies and subsidiaries, or legacy employee groups within merged organizations. While people may tolerate these differences in public, they will likely complain about them in private. When this occurs, you can create more effective collaboration by explicitly addressing and discussing the underlying sources of friction. Many times, you will find that topics people felt were taboo actually become quite harmless once they are brought into the light of day.

MISALIGNED CULTURES ACROSS BORDERS

BACKGROUND:
The North Atlantic region of a US-based marketing company consists of countries from UK and Western Europe which consistently encountered difficulties in coordinating the regional roll-out of products and services. I met with a group of representatives from each country to identify the roots of this problem.

WHAT THEY CALLED THE IDEA: "Regional Rollouts"

THE CULTURAL ISSUES:
Each nationality's long-held perceptions of the other began to leak into discussions of the rollout process. For example, the Italians thought the Germans wanted to impose too much structure on it. The Germans thought the French over-intellectualized the discussion about it. The French felt the Spanish approached the issue too casually. Most important, they all perceived the US executives as imperialistically imposing their ideas on them.

THE IMPACT OF THE CULTURAL MISALIGNMENT:
A lot of passive resistance began to creep into the conversation and it became impossible to come to a conclusion about almost anything. I gradually came to understand that the root of the problem had nothing to do with the idea of Rollouts but went back to the deeply-seated cultural resistance to the idea of a Homogenous North Atlantic Region. Once I recognized this, I encouraged each country to fine-tune the process for itself while retaining the integrity of the whole. The practical implications of these adjustments were minimal but allowed the group to deal with the underlying cultural conflict built into the idea of Regional Rollouts.

The global business environment presents a particular challenge to the Alignment of ideas. On one hand, a corporation's unique value to the international business community is maintained by the consistency of ideas about its policies, processes, products and services as they are held in the hearts and minds of its employees, customers and business partners. If these ideas weaken, the corporation weakens. A corporation is only as stable as the ideas that define it.

On the other hand, members of the global community demand the flexibility and diversity which allows a multinational corporation to respond to unique expectations and needs. In one country a person's word is as good as his bond; in another it is merely the opening gambit of a protracted negotiation. A friendly pat on the back in one culture is a rude insult in another. A flattened organization feels comfortably democratic in one political environment while it threatens the very fabric of society in another. How do you respond to these differences and yet maintain your organization's cultural and operational integrity?

The response of many organizations, when ideas rooted in different cultures conflict, is to ignore the differences as if they don't exist. This leads to a hypocritical environment in which people say one thing but do another. This, in turn, creates an intellectually dishonest atmosphere that devalues ideas in general. Another common approach is to systematically weed out the offending ideas by rewarding those whose ideas are in the mainstream and punishing those who are different. This results in an intellectually sterile environment. Other organizations avoid the problem by limiting the diversity of ideas through restrictive selection processes as individuals are initially hired or as they are chosen for key committees or prestigious assignments.

When cultural conflicts impinge on the effectiveness of your organization, it is most useful to address them directly. Help people to understand the issues by probing beneath the surface of the ideas and examining the roots of the discord. You will find that this intellectual honesty and openness regarding such conflicts strengthens your organization by limiting the loss of resources consumed when ideas are culturally misaligned. At the same time, the resulting clarity of thought and communication empowers individuals to capitalize on their diversity. This increases the likelihood that your idea achieves your organization's goals in the context of diverse cultures.

ALIGNMENT OF STRUCTURE

When I discussed the shape of ideas (see chapter 2) I explained how an idea that is structured with a degree of precision and not too many component parts is easy for people to pick up, to carry with them and to share with others. I explained how fuzzy or abstract ideas become concrete and practical when their structural elements are made clear. For example, financial reports make an organization's financial status very concrete. The structure of a project plan turns a variety of general intentions into a set of actionable tasks and clearly defined outcomes. A set of processes and tools, such as those used in Total Quality Management (TQM) or Six Sigma, converts the abstract idea of Quality into a substantive reality.

Unfortunately, having precise and simple structures does not guarantee the Alignment of two similar ideas. In fact, this can sometimes be a source of misalignment. For example, one of the challenges in a newly merged organization is that each group defines its ideas about quality, product development, or procurement in terms of the underlying processes and procedures it has traditionally used. If processes are structured similarly in each of the merged companies, they can be expected to mesh well with each other. If not—even if they are aligned in other ways—confusion will reign as the two groups attempt to collaborate. This problem is compounded when one group assumes that the lack of collaboration by the other is due to their unwillingness to work together rather than to differences in how they structure their ideas about the business issue.

The following example describes the differences in how a program manager (a manager of project managers) and a CFO in the same company approach the idea of Financial Status. Each structures the idea to fit their own perception of the work they do which inevitably leads to communication problems between them.

MISALIGNED STRUCTURES OF A FINANCIAL IDEA

BACKGROUND:
The new CFO of a mid-sized project-based engineering firm found it difficult to predict annual financial results because there was little relationship between how project managers and the CFO thought about financial status. Projects were generally of a duration of 6-18 months.

WHAT THEY CALLED THE IDEA: "Financial Status"

THE CFO'S STRUCTURE:
The CFO thought in terms of Income Statements and Balance Sheets that compared actual monthly numbers to budgeted numbers. This allowed her to project year-end financials based on the performance of different business units and to manage cash flow.

THE PROGRAM MANAGERS' STRUCTURE:
Program managers, as well as individuals running projects, thought about financial status in terms of a variety of project metrics generated by project management software. Some of these metrics were specific to the project type or even the project manager. They often were based on judgment calls such as estimates about exactly what percent of various aspects of the project were complete. This information, along with the experienced managers'

intuitive understanding of "how things work around here," allowed program managers to keep a finger on the financial pulse of the various projects. Program managers, in general, were more concerned about whether or not their projects would be completed within time and budget, which they usually were, than with precise financial reports during the course of their projects.

THE IMPACT OF THE MISALIGNMENT OF STRUCTURES:
While the project management software structured the idea of Financial Status in terms that mapped well to the project management process, they didn't map well to the corporate accounting system. The project managers were frustrated because they did not have the tools to convert their information to a structure the CFO found useful. As a result, the CFO could never be sure of the net impact of a project on the financial statements until the project, or major phases of it, was fully completed. This raised havoc with effective cash management. As the company grew larger, it was forced to do some major systems revisions to bring the two ideas of Financial Status in sync with each other.

Most people don't think very much about the impact that physical structures and even infrastructures of their organization—such as campuses, buildings and digital networks—have on how their ideas about the organization are structured, but they can be an important tool in creating Alignment. For example, the senior partners at Arthur Andersen, a major accounting firm (until it was dissolved), wanted their employees as well as their customers to think of their extended global partnership as "One Firm." They reinforced this idea by standardizing practices throughout the world, as most major accounting firms would. They also made sure that the same large double wooden doors of the original headquarters graced the entrance of every major office in the world. But it was the physical place referred to as "St. Charles" that most reinforced this One Firm identity. For many years, this was the one place in the world where every partner and every manager on the partner track was trained. The training could have been administered in offices all over the world, but it was held in the St. Charles learning center because it made the idea of One Firm concrete in a very literal way. I will return to the Arthur Andersen example in Chapter 4, where the erosion of the idea of One Firm led to a split in the partnership. Finally, I will also use it in Chapter 7 to demonstrate the idea of Organizational Culture and the challenge of balancing the tensions among values.

Think about your organization and others you know. How is information structured on its web page, intranet or knowledge base? How does this structure affect how you and others think about the organization? How about the physical relationship of executive offices to each other and to the rest of the organization? When different functions are housed in different buildings, does that influence your idea of how they work together? You will see that the physical as well as the conceptual structures that make up your organization have a strong effect on the ideas people hold about it—and how people interact with it.

Aligning ideas in terms of all four facets—Objectives, Culture, Vocabulary and Structure—helps to ensure that similar ideas mesh well with each other. To the extent that they don't mesh, these similar ideas will develop independently of each other as a function of the different mental and physical environments in which people work. As a consequence, you may find miniature versions of your idea sprouting up in organizational silos, and they will collectively have far less impact than if you could combine them into a single, integrated, high-momentum idea.

YOUR TURN

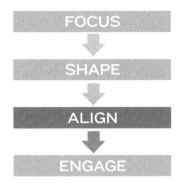

Step 3:
Align Your Idea for Synergy

This section guides you through a process of Aligning the Idea you identified at the beginning of the chapter. It includes:

DESCRIBE THE ALIGNMENT OF YOUR IDEA.

CONDUCT A SUCCESS FACTOR ANALYSIS OF YOUR IDEA.

CONDUCT A RISK FACTOR ANALYSIS OF YOUR IDEA.

IDENTIFY SPECIFIC ACTIONS TO STRENGTHEN THE ALIGNMENT OF YOUR IDEA.

Describe The Current Alignment
Of Your Idea

WHAT ARE YOU THINKING?

Before you conduct your Success Factor and Risk Factor Analyses on the following pages, take a moment to describe the current Alignment of your idea.

EXERCISE

1. List three other ideas in the organization that may be relevant to your idea.

2. Identify the degree to which each of these three ideas is aligned to the idea you have identified at the beginning of this chapter on each of the four facets of alignment, using the following code:

    A = The idea is aligned with yours (works with your idea)

    M = The idea is misaligned with yours (works against your idea)

    Blank = neutral or uncertain

Helpful Hint: Since there are thousands of ideas floating around in your organization that may help or hinder your idea, it may seem like a difficult task to identify just three. It is best to keep the list short for now, as you can always expand it later. Ask yourself, "What idea is out there that could get in the way of mine, or confuse people?" Or, "What is a related idea that already has the support of others that I can piggy-back on?"

OTHER IDEAS IN THE ORGANIZATION THAT MAY BE RELEVANT TO YOURS	OBJECTIVES	VOCABULARY	CULTURE	STRUCTURE

Success Factor Analysis: Alignment

The following pages describe five Success Factors that, if present, will maximize the momentum of your idea by leveraging that of similar ideas within the organization and minimizing the effect of those that may be in opposition to it.

SUCCESS FACTORS RELATED TO ALIGNMENT

3.1 A well-defined Future Vision

3.2 Long range idea scanning

3.3 An organization prepared to accept delivery of the idea

3.4 Integrated alignment processes

3.5 Intellectual honesty

The benefits of ensuring these Alignment-related Success Factors are in place include the following:

- The organization is less likely to be distracted and confused by multiple initiatives, projects or programs chasing similar ideas.
- Cross-organization alliances in support of an idea are more likely to occur, and political roadblocks are more likely to be identified and remedied before they become serious problems.
- People working on similar ideas or trying to achieve similar purposes are less likely to be blind-sided and react negatively to your idea when they stumble upon it.

As you review the Alignment-related Success Factors on the following pages, think about how they might apply to the idea you described on the previous page.

A WELL-DEFINED FUTURE VISION

The term "Future Vision" is usually used to refer to a CEO's idea of where the organization as a whole will be in a number of years and what it will look like. However it is equally useful in describing the idea the leader of any subordinate business unit has for the future of her area of responsibility. This, of course, should be aligned with the CEO's Future Vision as well as the Future Visions of any other executives between her and the CEO. The words "well-defined" mean that the Future Vision has been articulated in concrete terms and with meaningful metrics sufficient for leaders at successively lower levels in the organization to be sure their Future Visions are aligned with those above and below them.

The Future Vision of the organization, combined with the supporting Future Visions of its subordinate business units, comprise the organization's idea of itself. This big idea, to have maximum impact, must incorporate the same characteristics required for the success of ideas in general. In terms of Focus, as described in Chapter One, this means that the desired end results of the Future Vision must be defined well enough that the purpose, actors and actions of other ideas can be tested against them. In terms of Shape, as discussed in Chapter Two, the Future Vision must be more than a set of fuzzy hopes and dreams—it must be precise enough to provide direction while flexible enough to leave room for creativity. It must also be simple enough to avoid confusion while complex enough to provide a meaningful description of the anticipated future.

The most critical characteristic of a Future Vision is that it is a shared idea. If that idea is well-defined only in the heads of the leaders, it will be useless as a beacon for the Alignment of other ideas in the organization.

To what extent is this success factor in place?

☐ More than adequate
☐ Adequate
☐ Inadequate

LONG RANGE IDEA SCANNING

In order to take advantage of the momentum of related ideas within the organization a leader must be aware that multiple ideas with shared objectives and synergistic potential exist. I use the term "long range idea scanning" to emphasize that the further away you are in time, geography or organizational structure from a closely related idea, the less likely you are to be aware of it—and the more likely you are to waste organizational resources in promoting a redundant idea through the process of an initiative.

The due diligence required before investing resources in an idea must include this sort of environmental scanning. Most successful leaders have already developed this capability to allow them to take advantage of opportunities and avoid pitfalls. At the same time, it is all too easy for a creative, action-oriented leader to get so energized with an obviously useful idea that he fails to take the time to look for ideas with similar objectives already in motion, or about to be put into motion, in other parts of the organization.

Parallel ideas are best identified in the early stages of developing an idea. Searching for initiatives that have promoted similar ideas, past or current, will identify lessons learned and also potential supporters. Idea scanning can cover formal knowledge bases as well as information available through informal networks.

The biggest challenge to identifying parallel ideas across the organization is they are often hidden: They, or the problems they are intended to address, may be difficult to spot because they are perceived differently from different organizational or cultural perspectives, or the same ideas may be named or structured differently. For this reason, your scanning capability needs to penetrate beyond apparent walls and surfaces that may hide similar ideas from view.

To what extent is this success factor in place?

☐ More than adequate
☐ Adequate
☐ Inadequate

AN ORGANIZATION PREPARED TO ACCEPT DELIVERY OF THE IDEA

An idea delivered to an organization that is unprepared to receive it is likely to go to waste. Consider this analogous situation: The plant manager of a food manufacturing facility orders a special delivery of an unusual perishable commodity needed to fulfill a customer's one-time request. Unfortunately, no one on the loading dock was notified nor were the production staff who were on duty when the order arrived. Consequently, the delivery was refused and the perishable commodity went to waste.

Ideas are also perishable commodities. No matter how useful the idea is for the business, and no matter how efficient the initiative is in preparing the idea for delivery, if the organization is not prepared to receive it, the idea will sit on the loading dock waiting for the right people to realize its importance. Unfortunately, if an idea is allowed to sit around long enough without being used, its utility to the organization will diminish and those who might have found it useful will reject it because it has gone stale.

For an idea to be acceptable to the receiving organization, it must be aligned with existing ideas in terms of Objectives, Vocabulary, Culture and Structure. If the idea requires that people in the organization think about themselves or their work in ways different from what they are accustomed, preparation is particularly important. This includes involving people in the initiative process to develop and test the idea and otherwise move it forward. Most important, it includes gaining the trust of those you expect to accept the idea, before you drop it off unexpectedly on their loading dock.

To what extent is this success factor in place?

☐ More than adequate
☐ Adequate
☐ Inadequate

INTEGRATED ALIGNMENT PROCESSES

An alignment process is the mechanism by which those involved in an initiative keep in touch with each other as the idea is moved forward. For example, project management best practices dictate that any project should begin with a project alignment meeting attended by team members and stakeholders. The function of this meeting is to ensure basic assumptions are shared about the Objectives of the project, the Structure of the workflow, the Vocabulary to be used, and the like. It is also the time when a team culture begins to be established. However, Alignment cannot be a one-time event, but must be integrated with other project management processes typically used in carrying out an initiative.

In complex initiatives, it is challenge enough to maintain Alignment among team members and stakeholders regarding the hard facts of the initiative process. These might include specifications, timelines, resources and critical paths required to develop well-defined components necessary to introduce the idea to the organization—training, rollout events, or PR materials, for example. It is even more challenging to maintain Alignment about how people think about less well-defined aspects of the idea—such as the idea's purpose and expected impacts on the organization once the idea is accepted and integrated.

While the purpose and intended impact of an idea may be stated at the beginning of a project, these concerns tend to get lost in the shuffle of project activities. This is why processes need to be integrated into the initiative to continually align how the team and its stakeholders think about the big idea the initiative is expected to deliver—as well as how they perceive the initiative process that makes that delivery. This Success Factor emphasizes, once more, the need to differentiate between the process of delivering the idea to the organization and the idea itself.

To what extent is this success factor in place?

☐ More than adequate
☐ Adequate
☐ Inadequate

INTELLECTUAL HONESTY

Intellectual honesty means looking an idea straight in the face and asking tough questions about it so that misalignment issues can be addressed before they turn into operational issues. Early chapters in this book have suggested the nature of these questions: What is the purpose of the idea being forwarded by this initiative? What actions need to be taken by whom to accomplish this purpose? Is this idea going to be comprehensible to those who are expected to act on it? Is there substance behind its fuzzy edges? Has this idea been delivered to the organization before? Is someone else delivering it now? Since poorly conceived ideas can absorb momentum from other ideas, allowing them to be delivered to the organization can be a costly drain of scarce resources. This is why the tough questions should be posed early in the conception-to-delivery process.

Intellectual honesty requires that an idea not be taken at face value, even if it originates from the highest levels of the organization. For some people, having their ideas challenged feels very much like having their self worth questioned. Thus, challenging an idea at this level of detail can be politically or socially risky. In some organizations, there is a sort of quid pro quo understanding of "I won't challenge your ideas if you don't challenge mine." These are reasons people neglect to ask the tough questions, and by extension support each other in intellectual dishonesty – not exactly a recipe for success.

Intellectual honesty needs to start at the top. You, as leader, need to set the example of intellectual honesty by demanding that these tough questions be asked of your ideas by both peers and subordinates. The advantage of a framework for analyzing ideas, such as the one proposed in this book, is that this activity can become formalized and thus depersonalized.

Asking tough questions exposes underlying assumptions that people have taken for granted without knowing that others hold different assumptions. This, in turn, allows alignment issues to be dealt with at the conceptual stage rather than waiting for the momentum of the idea to be sapped later by parallel or conflicting ideas.

To what extent is this success factor in place?

- ☐ More than adequate
- ☐ Adequate
- ☐ Inadequate

The common theme of this chapter is that leaders often fail to take advantage of the momentum of other ideas in the organization, usually because they are simply unaware of them until it is too late.

RISK FACTORS RELATED TO ALIGNMENT

3.1 Double vision

3.2 Ships pass in the night

3.3 Ideas collide silently

3.4 The team insulates itself from stakeholders

3.5 Open warfare

Spotting these risk factors in a timely fashion and then taking appropriate actions to mitigate these risks will help you to avoid common Alignment-related failures such as the following:

- Experts involved with developing the initiative process have difficulty communicating with non-experts who don't have a firm grasp of the underlying principles that support the idea.

- The conceptual framework and vocabulary used to discuss the initiative, and the idea it supports, are so inconsistent across constituents that coordination and collaboration becomes difficult.

- People are unable to accept delivery of the idea simply because they can't get clear on what it represents or what they should do with it.

As you review the following risk factors, and the related risk indicators, think about ways in which you might adjust the alignment of your idea to meet the needs of those people who you wish to accept and act on it.

DOUBLE VISION

Double vision is what occurs when the Future Vision of the organization varies among two senior executives or their stakeholders to the extent that they are pulling against each other. Although they may be aware of their differences, often they are not and simply wonder why their significant combined resources don't provide equally significant results. The same thing happens on a smaller scale when an idea is being moved forward by an initiative but participants each hold different versions of that idea in their heads. A particularly disappointing form of double vision is when the people of the organization refuse to accept an idea because it bears no relevance to any vision they have of themselves or their work.

Even if the organization's leadership does hold a single Future Vision, if that vision doesn't make it into initiative team discussions about the long-term purpose of the idea they are charged with moving forward, that Future Vision cannot serve to align their efforts. The consequence is that those to whom they deliver the idea don't realize its significance for the future of the organization. They see the initiative as "just another irritation."

RISK INDICATORS

- ☐ The logical, long-term consequences of an initiative don't reflect the espoused Future Vision of the company.
- ☐ The underlying assumptions held by proponents of one or more initiatives are contradictory.
- ☐ When asked to describe the initiative, people on the same team come up with very different interpretations of what it is about.
- ☐ People give lip service to the official Future Vision of the initiative but act contrary to that vision.
- ☐ Employees dismiss a new idea as irrelevant to their work and their organization.

How important is this risk to your idea?
- ☐ Not important
- ☐ Important
- ☐ Critical

RISK MITIGATION: SEE SUCCESS FACTORS 3.1, 3.4 & 3.5.

SHIPS PASS IN THE NIGHT

I have sometimes interviewed employees about an initiative-in-progress only to discover that a similar project was already underway elsewhere in the organization. The two initiatives were rarely identical, but they commonly had large overlaps. People were often unaware of this redundancy because the initiatives originated in different parts of the organization and people used different vocabulary to refer to them. This was a particular problem when parallel initiatives were separated by gaps between organizational or geographic cultures. Sometimes the initiatives were created in response to different symptoms, even though the root problem was identical. In other cases, one of the projects was structured as an "organizational initiative," and the other was built into the normal evolution of existing processes and procedures. When ideas—or the initiatives that carry them forward—are invisible to each other, they are like 'ships passing in the night.'

The consequence of wasted resources is obvious, but this duplication of effort also yields confusion among employees and loss of confidence in the executives who don't realize the redundancy.

RISK INDICATORS

- ☐ Similar ideas are developed in multiple silos with their respective proponents unaware of the efforts of the other.
- ☐ Employees comment that "the left hand doesn't seem to be aware of what the right hand is doing."
- ☐ Stakeholders, being interviewed for a new initiative, report they were interviewed for a similar one earlier in the year.
- ☐ A business unit addresses an issue that is probably being faced by other business units, but neglects to check in with them.
- ☐ Heads of business units purposely keep certain initiatives below the corporate radar to protect their independence.

How important is this risk to your idea?

☐ Not important
☐ Important
☐ Critical

RISK MITIGATION: SEE SUCCESS FACTORS 3.1, 3.2 & 3.4.

IDEAS COLLIDE SILENTLY

Passive resistance, where people work against an idea in ways that are not obvious, is a risk anytime people haven't yet bought into it. When this happens, the project team or its sponsoring stakeholders may recognize that the idea they are moving forward is meeting resistance, but they are unable to identify the hidden barriers. These barriers may include alternative ideas that people support privately but that are never addressed in public discussions. For example, ideas such as the following often are held but not expressed in the face of a new idea: "This change is bad for the organization," or "This SVP doesn't understand the business at the ground level," or "This initiative is intended to reduce the need for my department." Each of these privately held ideas may be in direct opposition to the idea promoted by an initiative, but they are kept hidden under the surface for fear of retribution.

Silent resistance is a product of a culture that doesn't encourage dissent. When people are not allowed to express their disagreement—that their view of a situation does not align with that of others—ideas will remain on a collision course. Unfortunately, the danger won't be noticed until it is too late—and, even then, it might not be publicly discussed. When people are not allowed to challenge an idea with which they disagree, they are likely to find ways to deal with it passively. The collisions occur, but they occur silently.

RISK INDICATORS

- ☐ An idea stalls but it is unclear why.
- ☐ Key stakeholders don't show up at critical meetings.
- ☐ Resources pledged to support the initiative are delayed or withdrawn.
- ☐ People make public commitments of support that are inconsistent with their actions.
- ☐ Problems are put on the back burner by those whose participation is required for their solution.

How important is this risk to your idea?
- ☐ Not important
- ☐ Important
- ☐ Critical

RISK MITIGATION: SEE SUCCESS FACTORS 3.1, 3.2, 3.3 & 3.4.

THE TEAM INSULATES ITSELF FROM STAKEHOLDERS

Some people like to be involved in tightly defined projects or initiatives because of the clarity they provide through precisely stated objectives, tasks, timelines and resources. Inexperienced managers of initiatives sometimes use these specifications and plans as a protective wall that serves to keep pesky stakeholders from slowing them down with change requests or time-consuming status meetings. There is a lot of motivation to take this stance when the timelines are tight and the political costs of going beyond timeline or budget are significant.

The ideas held within a team that insulates itself from its customers and other stakeholders are likely to be highly aligned with each other. This, in fact, may enable them to carry out the process of an initiative in record time and under budget. However, remaining out of touch with the rest of the organization increases the risk of their misalignment with the ideas of customers and stakeholders. This is a particular danger when the environment around the project is changing. An initiative team that keeps its head in the sand remains ignorant of these sometimes subtle changes. Consequently, they may be unpleasantly surprised when the organization refuses to accept the idea the initiative was intended to deliver to it.

RISK INDICATORS

- ☐ Meeting formal specifications becomes more important than satisfying emerging needs of stakeholders.
- ☐ Initiative sponsors or other stakeholders are not invited to initiative team meetings.
- ☐ Team members thwart input by defensively referring to original specifications.
- ☐ Changing conditions and assumptions are ignored.
- ☐ Team discussions refer to themselves as "us" and to their stakeholders as "them."

How important is this risk to your idea?
- ☐ Not important
- ☐ Important
- ☐ Critical

RISK MITIGATION: SEE SUCCESS FACTORS 3.3 & 3.4.

OPEN WARFARE

Open disagreement with an idea is a good thing because it can lead to thoughtful discussions and revisions. Open disagreement assumes a mutual desire for a collaborative resolution to ideas that are not well aligned with each other.

On the other hand, open warfare occurs when people don't give up talking but do give up listening. Lines get clearly drawn and victory is defined by the annihilation of one or more of the opposing ideas. By the time open disagreement turns to open warfare, the discussion usually is no longer directly related to the idea itself but to some external ideas related to personalities, politics or greed.

The root cause of open warfare, in terms of ideas being moved forward by organizational initiatives, usually is that the warring stakeholders were not sufficiently involved in the early discussions to identify how their ideas were not aligned and what to do about it. Or maybe alignment discussions were never held, blindsiding everyone once it became clear what the idea required of its stakeholders.

RISK INDICATORS

- ☐ Discussions about priorities and resource allocations across initiatives become heated.
- ☐ Concerted efforts are made by factions within the organization to cancel the initiative.
- ☐ Executives and managers instruct their employees not to participate.
- ☐ Emails are used to attack or document positions rather than to resolve problems.
- ☐ Politics guide the realignment of an idea rather than purpose or vision.

How important is this risk to your idea?

- ☐ Not important
- ☐ Important
- ☐ Critical

RISK MITIGATION: SEE SUCCESS FACTORS 3.3, 3.4 & 3.5.

Thought-Provoking Questions
About The Alignment Of Ideas

You will find that it is easier to think about the risks addressed in this chapter, and to help others think about them, by asking questions. Use the following questions to inquire about one or more of the ideas you have considered in this chapter.

- Exactly how will this idea support our Future Vision? What string of cause-and-effect relationships connects the impact of this idea to our Future Vision? [Alignment with Future Vision]

- What other ideas have objectives that are similar or complementary to this one? What other ideas have objectives that are contrary to the objectives of this idea? What can you do to capitalize on the efforts of others or resolve potential conflicts? [Alignment of Objectives]

- What existing processes or procedures will need to be changed for this idea to work? How can you make that transition easy for people? How can you adjust the idea to minimize unnecessary changes? [Structural Alignment]

- What specific words or terms do you use to describe the key aspects of this idea? What other words could be used to describe the same thing? Who might be confused by your terminology? What are you doing to ensure everyone consistently uses the same terminology in the same way? [Alignment of Vocabulary]

- What groups of employees or other stakeholders view this idea as contrary to the way they view their work or their world? What changes will this idea require to how people are used to thinking or acting? How will you bridge those gaps? [Cultural Alignment]

NOW WHAT?

Review your assessment of the Success Factors and Risk Factors and indicate what actions, if any, are required to increase the effectiveness of your idea.

CHAPTER 4
Position Your Idea
for Engagement

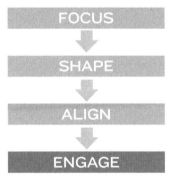

FOCUS

SHAPE

ALIGN

ENGAGE

STEP 4: ENGAGEMENT
IN A NUTSHELL

Your role as a leader is to anticipate the meaning employees will find in your idea by understanding the lenses they use to decide "What's In It For Me?" (WIFM) from non-monetary as well as monetary perspectives.

KEY POINTS

- Engagement describes the degree to which an idea engages the hearts, as well as the minds, of the people required to implement an idea. Engagement determines how much they will invest in it.

- An Employee views an idea through a set of personal lenses. He will engage with the idea depending on the answers to the questions that these personal lenses raise, including:

    Profession: How does this idea conform to my professional beliefs? Will it increase my value as a professional?

    Team: How will the idea strengthen my team and take advantage of what it has to offer? Will it threaten our value as a team?

    Organization: Is this idea consistent with the idea of the organization as I know it? How does it conform to the explicit or implied commitments it has made to me?

    Personal Values: How well does this idea conform to my beliefs about ethics, morality, philosophy, politics, religion and related concerns?

    Family: How will this idea affect my ability to support my family? Will it elevate their perception of my role in the organization?

    Society: How will this idea affect the world around me? Will it contribute to what I value in society or detract from it?

PUT YOUR STAKE IN THE GROUND

The purpose of this very brief exercise is to encourage you to apply what you read in each chapter to a situation of your own. You may use the same idea you used for this purpose in one of the previous chapters, or you may want to identify another idea for this chapter.

EXERCISE

Describe how you refer to your idea:

Give a short name or phrase you would use in normal conversation when discussing this idea. For example, it might be a single word, such as "Mentoring" or "Blog," or a phrase such as "Reducing Waste through Six Sigma."

Identify the 2-3 processes you will use or (have used / are using) to deliver this idea to the organization:

You will find it most useful if you can identify 2-3 more specific processes, such as:

- *"The development of a social/professional group consisting of high potential employees slated for the fast track."*
- *"Develop a mentoring program for employees on the fast track."*
- *"Create an internal chat room in which employees can voice their concerns."*

THE VOLUNTEER EMPLOYEE

What if you knew your employees would perform only on their own volition without any kind of compensation? What if you didn't pay them a salary, but simply waited for them to volunteer for the tasks they preferred to take on? What if they carried out their job responsibilities only if they wanted to? What if they supported and implemented your ideas only when they found them to be personally meaningful?

Some leaders expect that if they deliver an idea to an employee, she will accept and act on it because that's what she gets paid for. In actuality, much of the important work in organizations is done on a voluntary basis. Think about it. Most people in organizations can do their jobs by operating at 80% of their actual capacity, receiving full salary and even advancing regularly. This means that your employees provide the remaining 20% only when they find their work so meaningful that they take personal ownership of it—when they commit themselves to doing whatever it takes to achieve success. In the field of organizational development, this state of mind is called "Engagement." This additional excitement and engaged mental energy represents a valuable organizational resource that you, as a leader, can leverage. This chapter will show you how to engage your people so they actively help power your ideas through to the results that you want. Harnessing that 20% can make the difference between an interesting place to work that attracts and retains the best talent, and a run-of-the-mill organization that settles for second-best. When you engage this additional 20%, you and your people will beat out the competition through more innovative products, efficient work processes, committed employees, satisfied customers and, yes, more successful projects and organizational initiatives.

Any idea begins as a conception and moves through an organization until it comes to its final stop in the heads of those who must act on it. Acceptance of the idea is key—if the persons expected to act on the idea do not accept its delivery, they will not take the actions required to provide the anticipated results. To build Engagement, you need to understand how to deliver your idea effectively to different people who see your idea from different perspectives. The process that delivers this idea can enhance the likelihood of its acceptance, or it can diminish it to the point that it has no impact.

The Executive Review Panel indicated that the lack of commitment of employees is a common characteristic of the failed initiatives they had observed over the previous ten years, as illustrated in the following graph.

FOR THOSE INITIATIVES THAT FAILED TO HAVE A SIGNIFICANT IMPACT, HOW OFTEN WERE THE APPROPRIATE EMPLOYEES COMMITTED TO THE INITIATIVE?

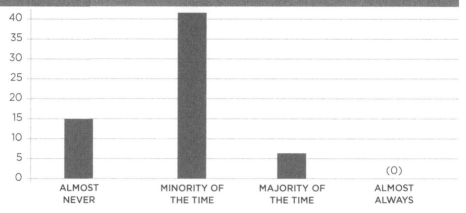

When you decide to promote an idea within your organization, you face a battle for position and 'mind share' in the minds of your employees, colleagues and bosses. It doesn't matter whether it is an idea about your strategic vision, an improved process, a revised organizational structure or simply an idea about how an employee can improve his performance. The clutter of competing ideas is just as great, the ability of the human mind to absorb information and focus attention is just as limited, and the din of information is just as overpowering as it is in the commercial marketplace. Product marketers live in this kind of environment and they understand the principle of voluntary behavior because their job is to convince potential customers to volunteer not only their time and effort, but their money as well, to purchase their products. A marketer's most important goal is to position the idea of the product so that customers perceive a relationship between that idea and how they prefer to view themselves, their history and especially their future—and how they would like others to view them.

You are in the same position. You cannot force or coerce employees into voluntarily giving their additional 20% of commitment, interest and drive, at least not for long. Employees soon burn out, give up or leave. This kind of support for your idea can only be given by the employee out of personal choice, i.e., voluntarily. So here's the key point: an employee will become truly engaged with your idea only when he is able to connect it with his view of himself. He needs to connect with your idea in terms of what he values and how he sees his role in the organization and in society. The more he can see congruence between your idea and what he values most, the more likely he is to volunteer his time and effort to support it.

For example, a respected consulting firm attracts the brightest and the best of young professionals. Its leaders want to identify and put on the fast track the most promising of these as future leaders of the organization. To accomplish this, they need to deliver to these high potential employees the idea that the organization provides opportunities for long-term professional advancement to those willing to make a personal commitment to the organization. The firm delivers this idea through an initiative called, "Lead On," a voluntary after-hours professional development group managed by the young employees themselves. Within the group, those most willing and able to become strong leaders recognize the value of voluntarily taking on increasing levels of responsibility to contribute to the group—and they do so. Thus, the idea of Growth through Commitment, as delivered through the process of the Lead On initiative, serves as a self-selection device for the fast track program. Those employees who perceive the idea as important to their own values and goals demonstrate their acceptance of that idea by actively contributing to the group. Those who choose not to accept delivery of the idea and, thus, do not actively contribute to the group, essentially remove themselves from the fast track leadership program.

In any organization, different individuals have different value systems—and different ways of evaluating whether congruence exists or not between your idea and their values. I refer to these systems as 'lenses,' and this chapter will teach you about six lenses that employees can use to evaluate your idea as it is delivered to them. If you understand these lenses you will be able to increase the likelihood that your idea will appeal to different individuals with different value systems. I'll describe strategies you can use to help employees and other stakeholders understand why they should care about your idea, how you can help them to find personal meaning in it. The phrase, "personal meaning" may seem very abstract and soft. However the six lenses provide a concrete framework for thinking about how employees evaluate an idea. Understanding how they perceive your idea enables you to position it for their engagement. At the close of the chapter, I will give you some practical tips for promoting Engagement and becoming the kind of leader who is able to engage the hearts and minds of the stakeholders whose support is most needed.

SIX PERSONAL LENSES

Employees and other stakeholders will always evaluate your idea by asking the question, consciously or unconsciously, "Why should I care?" The smart leader understands that an employee's answer to this question involves more than salary and bonus. When an employee volunteers that additional 20% of effort, it's because of what is personally meaningful to her. No two employees will find the same meaning in any one of your ideas. Nevertheless, you can anticipate the meaning employees will find in your idea by understanding the lenses they look through to evaluate it.

Each of the six lenses address a different set of issues, and when you view your idea from these varied perspectives, you will come face-to-face with the reality that your idea can't be all things to all people. However, you can encourage all people to find their own personal meaning in your idea—to connect the dots between your idea and what is important to them. Sometimes there may be substantial overlap among employees in an organization with a consistent culture or who come from similar origins, and this can make your job easier. In organizations that have more variability, working one-on-one with individuals, or mentoring or coaching them, may be the most effective way of helping them to see this connection; but you also need to know how to do this from a distance when it is impossible to meet every individual personally.

PAST ➡ PRESENT ➡ FUTURE

THE SIX LENSES OF ENGAGEMENT

LOOKING THROUGH THE PROFESSIONAL VALUES LENS

Ask a doctor, a lawyer, an IT expert or an engineer what she does for a living. If she names her profession before she names her company or what role she plays in it, she will most likely view your idea through her professional lens. Many who have formal professional credentials value those degrees and certifications because of the resources they have devoted to achieving and maintaining them. More significantly, they may have chosen their profession because they personally identify with its values or its approach to thinking and problem solving. They probably have been part of the profession before they joined your organization and they most likely plan to be a part of it after they leave.

People who view the world through their Professional Values lenses define themselves by the knowledge, skills and insights they carry with them from one employer to another. Professionals, especially those in early or mid-career, often will evaluate your idea from the perspective of what it will do for their career growth. On the other hand, some professionals, particularly experts, may be able to evaluate your ideas only through their Professional Values lens. They may be so steeped in their area of expertise that they can't stand back to see the big picture of the larger organization and its issues. These are factors you need to take into account when you wish to engage employees who view your idea through the lens of their professional identity.

PROFESSIONAL VALUES LENS: EXAMPLE 1

Jackie was recently promoted to the position of General Counsel for a large construction firm. She decided to launch an initiative she called "Focused Expertise," as a means for more efficient processing of cases. She expected her idea to be well received by the attorneys reporting directly to her since their bonuses were dependent on the number of cases completed. The core component of her new idea was to compartmentalize the work of her employees so that each would become very agile in resolving issues in a particular specialty—they would rarely have to get involved in issues outside of that area of expertise. As a result, efficiency did go up for many of the attorneys. However, morale took a dive, particularly among her most promising young attorneys. Several who had previously been willing to do whatever it takes to get a job done began to restrict their efforts to the necessary 80%. Some asked for transfers to other parts of the organization. Clearly, her idea for staff specialization, as delivered through her Focused Expertise initiative, was not being accepted as she had hoped.

Jackie discovered the problem when she had a conversation with David, a high-potential staff attorney. He told her that the reason he had accepted a job at the company was the opportunity it would provide him to broaden and deepen his professional knowledge and skills. While the initiative may have contributed to increased staff efficiency and even larger bonuses, when the youngest and brightest viewed the idea of Focused Expertise through their professional lenses, they could only see lost developmental opportunities.

Fortunately, Jackie had established a trusting relationship and open communications with her staff, and she was able to alleviate potential problems by aligning her idea with the professional values of her group. In the next example the leader had to break through an even tougher barrier: cynicism.

PROFESSIONAL VALUES LENS: EXAMPLE 2

Catherine was the head of product development for a division of a global electronics manufacturer. She realized that her engineers needed to collaborate more effectively—not only with their fellow product developers around the globe, but with everyone else who contributed to getting the product on the shelves before the competition. She realized that the biggest problem she faced was selling the value of the very non-technical sounding idea of Collaboration to a large group of professional engineers. As a group, they had a history of dismissing ideas related to interpersonal skills as inherently non-technical. One engineer cynically proclaimed, as he examined the idea of Collaboration through his lens of hard facts and logical reasoning, "Soft skills are as useful as soft data!" For him, this point of view was part of his personal and professional identity.

Catherine dealt with this challenge in two ways. First, she hired a consultant to interview successful design engineers within the organization and to create a data-base of their responses. These included actual quotes, tips, case studies and other information describing the practical benefits of collaboration. Created by engineers, for engineers, this data base was made broadly accessible. It became a point of honor to be included in it. Second, she brought together a team of engineers, and some instructional design consultants, to create a simulation game. This game was embedded with a complex cause-and-effect model of the relationship between specific collaborative behaviors and project success. Success in the game was defined by three concrete metrics: Development cost, time to market, and quality. I observed a pilot of this game in which teams of engineers crowded around computer terminals, intensely engaged in competition to figure out the underlying cause-and-effect model.

Catherine might have delivered the idea of Collaboration by plopping it on the desks of her engineers in the form of a set of policies or even a training program entitled "The Benefits of Collaboration." However, she knew that previous ideas delivered in that manner were rejected almost immediately as "another one of those ideas promoted by the human resources group." Catherine got the engagement she wanted by enabling the product engineers to draw the dots between the collaborative behaviors she was promoting and the project outcomes they valued as engineers. Because Catherine viewed her idea of Collaboration through the fact-based and logical orientation of the professional lenses of her design engineers, she gained acceptance of it.

Employees such as Catherine's product development engineers see themselves as professionals first and employees second. They view you, your organization and the work you give them through the lens of their profession. You will increase the probability employees will accept your idea if you can involve them in both its design and delivery. The easiest way to engage them in your idea is to ask them, 1) what they see in it from their professional perspectives; and, 2) what you can do to increase the likelihood of its acceptance by them and their colleagues.

LOOKING THROUGH THE TEAM LENS

Members of strong, integrated teams will view your idea through a shared Team Lens. These people find personal meaning in their collegial relationships and in the personal and professional value each contributes to the team. You may see members of such teams giving each other high fives to celebrate their successes. They may create team social events or even wear team T-shirts. In times of organizational strife, they may support their team with a passion even after they have lost faith in the larger organization.

Team members will evaluate your idea through their shared Team Lens to assess the meaning it has for the team as a whole. They will seek to determine if your idea elevates them, challenges them, celebrates them, or otherwise reinforces the image they have of themselves. They also will judge whether or not your idea presents a barrier to what they are trying to accomplish as a team. If your idea threatens them, they may look for a means of avoiding it or rebelling against it. In the same way, engaging a cohesive team with your idea can propel it forward. However, if team members don't see the relationship your idea has with their team identity or purpose, that same team cohesion can act on your idea as a dragging anchor.

TEAM LENS: EXAMPLE 1

An extreme example of a team's rebellion against a core corporate idea occurred in the 1980s within the emerging consulting practice of Arthur Andersen, the "Big Five" accounting firm to which I referred in the previous chapter.

Here's a little background: Since Arthur Andersen was founded in 1913, its primary focus was to provide audit and accounting services to major corporations. By the 1980s, all major CPA firms were experiencing price competition from increasing numbers of smaller firms. As a result, consulting groups developed within the traditional large accounting firms as a means of creating new revenue streams. These groups began to provide services beyond those of public accounting such as providing their clients with advice on how to build or run their businesses.

During that period, I was asked to audit the evaluation processes used by Arthur Andersen's

St. Charles training center to assess the quality of their own educational programs. As part of this process, I interviewed partners from all service lines within the firm, including the emerging consulting group. I will refer to it here as the consulting team.

Even at that time, it was clear that a separate culture was evolving within the consulting team that caused them to think of themselves as different from the rest of the organization. In particular, they were proud of the fact that their team achieved significantly larger profit margins than the traditional audit-related service lines. However, this team perspective conflicted with one of the strongest ideas traditionally held by the partners of the organization—the "One Firm" concept—and became the root cause of an eventual split in the partnership.

The "One Firm" concept—the idea of the partners being "all for one, and one for all," had been a core value of the organization since its inception. However, the Team Lens used by the emerging consulting services group began to provide quite a different view. When the consulting team looked at the larger organization through their Team Lens, they no longer saw "One Firm," but, rather a firm that was different from their team. That's when the rebellion began, starting with behind-the-scenes conversations about perceived inequities. These were soon followed by formal requests by the consulting team members for a greater share of profits. Finally, in the ultimate act of rebellion, the consulting team felt so strongly about their differences, based on what they saw through their Team Lens, that they split off from the partnership. Initially, they called themselves Andersen Consulting and, later, as they became a public company, Accenture.

This example shows the power of the Team Lens when it is used to view an idea. Perhaps the "One Firm" concept had outlived its usefulness and the leadership could have done nothing to stop the consulting group from rejecting that idea. Or, perhaps, looking through that group's Team Lens far in advance of the breakup might have allowed the senior partners to anticipate the problem and develop some alternatives.

TEAM LENS: EXAMPLE 2

A document management software firm has an excellent product that deals with keeping track of documents for the legal departments of large companies. The CEO decided to make the product much more robust and powerful by acquiring a dozen software firms, each of which provided document management solutions for other organizational functions. He stipulated a key criterion for acquisition was that a target company must have a very strong sales team. His intent was to integrate the various products into a single, enterprise-wide document management system with a unified sales force. He called his idea "the integrated solution."

His idea faced a challenge. On one hand, the sales teams of each of the acquired companies were passionately committed to the success of their individual products. For example, one team focused on helping marketing organizations keep track of materials supplied by multiple vendors, another sold to construction and engineering groups to help them manage their project documentation, another offered document security solutions to IT groups, and so forth. On the other hand, no team had any passion for the other products acquired through acquisition.

The CEO and his executive team actively promoted the idea of The Integrated Solution throughout the sales organization, the goal being that they would use that idea to position their product line with senior executives of their customer's organizations. This was in contrast to the normal practice of teams pitching their individual products at lower levels. Unfortunately, each sales team was most comfortable selling their own legacy products and found it distracting to themselves and their customers to introduce an idea that promoted the value of other products. They were willing to volunteer that extra 20% for their own team's wares, but not for any others. When each viewed the idea of The Integrated Solution through their original Team Lenses, they saw the other products as competitors rather than partners.

Fortunately, the CEO understood what the world looks like through the lens of a sales team dedicated to its product. Therefore, he recognized the problem and developed a way to deliver the idea of The Integrated Solution in a way that developed engagement across teams. First, he built an extensive training program that helped sales reps to 1) Understand the function and business benefits of each other's products; and, 2) Understand how the products worked together to increase individual revenues through cross-selling. Then, the CEO invested in several national sales meetings designed to foster mutual respect and create a powerful sense of an integrated company. One of the most popular events was in a game show format. This required contestant groups, each composed of members from multiple product teams, to compete with each other to identify opportunities for an integrated sale. These events lead to shared respect among the sales teams and a mutual understanding of the value of the idea of The Integrated Solution. This was possible only because the CEO was able to view his idea through the unique lens of each original product team.

Both examples illustrate how an engaged and passionate team can hold an idea back or propel it forward—depending on how it perceives the relationship of the idea to the team. In the case of the Arthur Andersen consulting group, the team identity became so strong that they saw themselves as separate from the larger organization and no longer felt a need to support the "one firm" idea. In the case of the software company, the CEO was able to see the powerful but separate identity of each product team, and to devise a method of delivering his idea that engaged that power with a single, unified idea—the "integrated solution." This is a balancing act every leader of an organization faces. The self images of individual teams, functions or even business units can be powerful sources of energy. But, without engaging them all in a unified idea of the purpose of the organization, and its strategy, those teams can become silos that compete for resources and resist collaboration. While these silos may not formally split off from the rest of the organization, strong team identities maintained at the expense of a unified organizational focus can be similarly dysfunctional. Viewing your ideas through the lenses of individual teams can help you with this balancing act.

LOOKING THROUGH THE ORGANIZATION LENS

People examine your idea from their Organizational Lens to see if it is consistent with the idea of the organization as they know it. Employees acquire this lens from the stories and myths about the organization's origin, how it got where it is, and why people can be proud to be part of it. Some of these stories are consciously created by the organization, but most evolve as part of its culture. For example, Federal Express has the story of the driver who unbolted the drop-off box from its foundation and took it back to the terminal because he couldn't unlock it to retrieve his customers' packages. Southwest Airlines has stories about the jokes cracked by their flight attendants and pilots. McDonald's has stories about floor sweepers who advanced in the ranks to become senior executives with catsup in their veins.

Employees who think of your organization as their own and want to be a part of it for the long term will depend on their Organizational Lens when they evaluate your idea. They will want to know if your idea reinforces the pride they have in their organization or if it detracts from it. If, in the delivery of your idea, you can clarify the link between it and their positive perception of the organization, they will tend to give it the benefit of the doubt.

ORGANIZATION LENS: EXAMPLE 1

When I consulted with Motorola in the 1990s, employees had a strong sense of organizational pride rooted, in part, in their reverence for its chairman and chief executive, Robert Galvin—the son of the founder—and his hand-picked successor, Chris Galvin. When employees viewed ideas offered by the executive team through their organizational lens, they expected to see something positive. The Galvins wished to ensure the idea of Leadership at Motorola that had brought success to the organization over three generations was dispersed throughout the Motorola culture.

To effectively deliver this idea, they sponsored an initiative that required all personnel who had been promoted to at least a second-level management position to participate in a multi-day course called "Manager of Managers." This course was given only at the world headquarters campus, and it always included a 2-hour session with someone from the C-suite, often Robert or Chris Galvin himself. The intent of the course was to allow the younger managers to view the idea of Leadership at Motorola through a very powerful organizational lens, as members of the senior leadership team themselves held it up to their eyes for them.

The above example describes an organization with a long-established idea of itself. The following comes from a much younger organization whose idea of itself is in flux.

ORGANIZATION LENS: EXAMPLE 2

Tim, a 5-year employee at Yahoo, was filled with pride and self-respect when he was hired straight out of college. Among his friends who also applied to Yahoo, he was the only one who made it through the entire interview process. He knew Yahoo by its reputation and admired its freewheeling entrepreneurial culture, as well as its support of individual initiative. However, he had an idea-shattering experience when, in 2013, the new CEO abruptly delivered a new idea: She suddenly announced an end to telecommuting. Viewed through his Organizational Lens, the idea of Telecommuting represented not merely a personal convenience, but a spirit of freedom and mutual trust. For Tim, its termination—particularly with little apparent input from individual employees—stood in stark contrast to the idea he had of the company for which he had already developed a sense of ownership. Looking through the lens of the organization as he knew it, he felt betrayed. Though a valued contributor, Tim now had second thoughts about working there.

Your people use their Organizational Lens to understand how your idea fits into their view of the business as a whole. Even loyal employees will resist change if they perceive it as contradicting their perception of the organization they have come to know and respect. On the other hand, if employees can connect the dots between your idea and their perception of the organization they value, they will be energized to go the extra mile when carrying it forward. Therefore, when you deliver a new idea to your organization, include this factor in your change management strategy to circumvent the misunderstandings and minimize the resistance of the type encountered by the Yahoo CEO.

As a leader, you need to keep in touch with what your employees see through their Organizational Lens to help you understand how they will react to your idea. One way to do this is through the use of employee engagement surveys or reading the unofficial sites employees use to talk about your organization. However, it is probably most useful simply to take the time to chat with your employees about the company and the changes they wish to see, and to encourage your managers to do the same.

LOOKING THROUGH THE PERSONAL VALUES LENS

An employee's Personal Values Lens is based on beliefs about ethics, morality, philosophy, politics, religion and related concerns. Although these values have their roots in the families in which individuals were raised, they also reflect the experiences of adulthood. This is a sometimes touchy topic, because many people consider their beliefs and values to be private and, in some instances, it may be inappropriate to discuss them in the workplace.

Nevertheless, as an employee looks at your idea through the lens of his personal values, he notes if it is consistent with, neutral, or contradictory to his personal beliefs. His assessment, and the degree of perceived match or mismatch, will influence his decision to actively support your idea, ignore it or even subvert it.

PERSONAL VALUES LENS: EXAMPLE 1

A global bank purchased a small, Midwest regional bank and replaced the current president with Paul, an SVP of their own. Almost immediately, Paul launched an initiative to promote his idea of expanding the products and services used by each customer. He delivered his idea through the process he called "The Full Service Initiative." Its key components included training on cross-selling for all customer-facing personnel, from tellers to private bankers. For example, tellers were to suggest to customers with high balances in their checking account to speak with a private banker, and were even given daily quotas for doing so. Paul had used the same approach in several other acquisitions with great success. He was, therefore, surprised when local bank personnel resisted his idea. Even after increasing the bonuses and firing some of the underperformers, people were still not meeting their quotas.

Eventually, Paul was replaced by Laura, a senior executive from the original bank. Laura understood the validity of the idea of expanding the products and services used by each customer, but also understood the source of employee resistance to it. Looking through the lens of the personal values of her employees, a lens she herself shared, she knew that employees saw the emphasis on cross-selling as a violation of one of their most basic values: service to customers and the community. For many, this personal belief in the value of customer service is what attracted them to their employer when they first signed on. It also kept many working there, even when offered higher paying positions elsewhere. This deeply seated belief had its roots in earlier decades when the bank shared the risk of economic downturns with its customers, and supported the community when no one else was able to do so. For the current employees, these values reflected more than the corporate culture. They represented what they sincerely believed as individuals. Thus, they felt that the idea promoted through the process of The Full

Service Initiative required them to reject this basic personal value by foisting off on their customers products and services they didn't really need.

Laura recognized that there was a more effective way of delivering the idea of Full Service to her employees, one that took their personal values into account. Her first response was to let her employees know that she recognized this conflict. This in itself diffused some of the tension because her employees now felt they were being heard. However, the real impact came when she assembled teams to analyze the demographics of the banks customers and ask the question, "Which of these customers can truly benefit from one or more of the products and services we have to offer?" It became clear to employees that, by being selective about what they sold to whom and by aggressively pursuing those opportunities, they could actually increase their ability to serve their customers. To further build on this perspective, Laura adjusted the bonus structure to include a monthly award for the branch that came up with the best example of genuinely helping a customer reach his financial goals. These cases, in turn, were fed to the regional marketing group for use in its ad campaign. The result was a commitment to the idea of expanding the products and services used by each customer. The reason the legacy employees were now engaged with the idea was because Laura had viewed the idea through the lens of their personal values and then helped them to see its connections to those values.

The above example describes personal values shared by a group of people. The following shows how a manager dealt with a single individual who was uncomfortable with an idea as she viewed it through her personal lens.

PERSONAL VALUES LENS: EXAMPLE 2

Ken heads up the satellite data analysis division of a firm that sells information on global warming to agricultural companies. He needed to communicate a new idea to the members of his team: "We need to expand the company's market to include customers in the oil and gas industry." He promoted this idea through an initiative he called the "Product Enhancement Program." It involved tweaking current products and services to meet the needs of these new customers. He knew this would be a difficult idea for many of his employees to accept because they viewed the petroleum industry as an enemy of the environment.

Carol is one of these employees. She holds an advanced degree in environmental science and is passionate about climate change. Her boss knew that Carol, one of his strongest employees, viewed her work primarily through that lens of her personal values. He anticipated that she would have a very negative knee jerk reaction to the idea of serving the oil and gas industry as she viewed it from her perspective on climate change.

Knowing this, Ken took care in how he delivered the idea to Carol. He had a conversation with her, in advance, to let her know that he anticipated and understood her conflict. At the same time, he helped her think through her career goals and the potential for achieving them within the current organization. They agreed that she would not be directly involved in any oil and gas projects if she chose not to. At the same time, she would consider the possibility that the work they get from that industry would actually help those new customers move toward decreasing their contribution to global warming. If that didn't work for her, he would help Carol find a job elsewhere. Carol agreed to give it a try.

In these examples, personal values dominated as the employees made judgments about the new ideas. In the case of the bank employees, they didn't like what they saw through their lens of serving customer needs, until the new leader was able to place the idea in a more positive light. She did this by clarifying the connections between the ideas promoted by The Full Service Initiative and what the employees valued. In Carol's case, the boss's awareness of her Personal Values Lens enabled him to anticipate her negative reaction to the idea of marketing to the oil and gas industry and discuss it with her. The simple act of acknowledging and showing respect for an employee's values when they are conflict with the idea you are delivering to them will at least buy you some time for negotiating a solution.

I acknowledge that an employee's privacy needs to be respected—prying into their personal values if they don't want to discuss them is impolite and often unethical. However, sometimes managers use privacy as an excuse for avoiding difficult discussions, hoping they will go away if they are ignored. Sometimes these values are hidden just beneath the surface. For example, I once coached two very bright and very opinionated executives. They constantly butted heads because they each devalued anyone who immediately pushed back with a knee-jerk reaction whenever a strong opinion was expressed—even though each did that very thing themselves. It took only a few sessions for these two executives to realize they shared this counterproductive and rather negative value and, finally, to discuss it between themselves. What had been a very sensitive personal issue became an unimportant one, once they each understood this shared personal value and could even joke about it.

When unspoken conflicting personal values cause friction, they develop into larger issues that accumulate like a herd of elephants in the room that everyone sees but no one acknowledges. This results in a clumsy and unhelpful business environment. Understanding how employees view your idea through their personal lens will sometimes explain behavior that might otherwise appear to be irrational.

LOOKING THROUGH THE FAMILY LENS

When employees view your idea through their Family Lens, they will consciously or unconsciously ascertain if it poses any threat to their ability to support their loved ones. Some will wonder how it affects their family's perceptions of their value as partner or parent—or their family's pride in their success. They will also consider the very practical implications of your idea, such as what effect it will have on the amount and quality of time they will have to spend with their families.

Sometimes the answers to these questions are obvious, as when your idea affects compensation, work hours or amount of travel. Other times, both the questions and the answers are hidden deeper in their psyches, and employees may experience your idea positively or negatively without their direct awareness of why. For instance, a minor department reorganization might result in a change of an employee's job title from assistant director to senior manager, with no impact on compensation, responsibilities, number of direct reports or any other trappings of success. Nevertheless, he may feel uneasy about informing his spouse or children of the change because he fears they may see it as a lesser title.

As in the case of all six lenses, the view through the Family Lens may not seem logical to someone looking from their own perspective. Nevertheless, this does not make that view any less meaningful to the employee who owns and values that particular lens.

FAMILY LENS: EXAMPLE 1

Pam is the head of operations for a mid-sized marketing firm. The company's profit margins are being squeezed by low-cost competitors and the CEO has introduced the idea he calls "Going the Extra Mile" to encourage people to do their best to deal with this challenge. To emphasize her boss's message, Pam makes positive comments when she sees cars already in the employee parking lot when she herself arrives early. She also gives verbal pats on the back to employees still at their terminals in the late evening hours.

Jim, on the other hand, is a very solid nine-to-five worker in the graphics art department. He appreciates the idea of Going the Extra Mile, because he recognizes the competitive challenges his company is facing. At the same time, he views everything in his life through his Family Lens and chooses to forget his job once he walks out the door at quitting time and doesn't want to be reminded of it until he walks back in. So, when he viewed the idea of Going the Extra Mile through his Family Lens, he resisted seeing it as a demand for volunteered hours through longer work days—as many of his colleagues interpreted that idea. Rather, he saw it as a requirement for increased efficiency and productivity on his part. Consequently, he responded to the idea by managing his time more effectively, carrying on fewer informal conversations with co-workers, cutting back on break times and the like.

Unfortunately, Jim's superiors confused his unwillingness to extend his hours with a lack of commitment to the idea of Going the Extra Mile, and passed him up when it came time to hand out bonuses or consider him for a promotion. They should have looked at the idea through the very consistent perspective of his family lens. The following example shows how the family lens may not always be so consistent and can change with new circumstances.

FAMILY LENS: EXAMPLE 2

Of the six lenses, the Family Lens is the one that can most easily change over time. Nancy is the SVP for HR at a global engineering and construction firm. Several years ago, she introduced an idea she characterized as "work-life balance." A defining aspect of this idea was the three-day weekend that took the form of a mandatory Monday- through-Thursday work week with 10-hour days. Most employees embraced the idea. Laurie and her long-term boyfriend Howie, who work for the same company, considered this a boon because it allowed them to take extended weekend camping trips.

However, once Laurie and Howie got married and started a family, both of them began to view the idea of Work-Life Balance through a revised and enhanced Family Lens. Instead of seeing long weekend trips, they now saw a limitation on the quality time they could spend each day with their child, not to mention a limitation on their hours of sleep. Both were valued employees, but unless Nancy could view the idea of Work-Life Balance through the Family Lens of new parents and expand it to include other options, such as job sharing or flex time, she risked losing Laurie and Howie to her competitors—and being unable to attract people like them in the first place.

These examples demonstrate how a seemingly good idea can elicit very different responses, depending on the view through each employee's Family Lens. The case of Laurie and Howie illustrates how taking the family perspective into account poses a particular challenge because the Family Lens changes as family circumstances change. Getting a firm fix on an employee's preferences by looking through this lens may require tracking a moving target. When Jim viewed his boss Pam's idea of Going the Extra Mile through his Family Lens, he responded by working more efficiently. Unfortunately, Pam didn't notice the increased efficiency and assumed that Jim was refusing to cooperate because of the value he placed on his family time. If she had taken the time to talk to Jim about how he actually viewed her idea through his Family Lens, she would have learned something about how margins could be increased without employees feeling the need to come early and stay late to show their commitment. She would also see the value of providing praise or other rewards to this profit enhancing employee.

As a leader, you may not always be able to adjust your idea, or its delivery, to conform to the needs of individual families. However, trying to see your idea through the Family Lens may help you to minimize potential conflicts and will also demonstrate to your employees that you value this perspective. Also, by getting them involved in the conversation, you may come up with some useful alternatives.

LOOKING THROUGH THE SOCIETY LENS

People look through their Society Lens to answer the question, "What am I doing to make this a better world?" This lens is, of course, important to employees of non-profit organizations who take the job because of the opportunity to make a social contribution. But, many people in for-profit organizations also ask this question and will be pleased if they see how their work creates a benefit to society.

Employers deal with this need by creating fund raising or community support activities, by matching employee donations to their favorite charities, or providing other civic support. But some miss the opportunity to help employees understand the ways in which they contribute to society merely by providing the products and services they are employed to produce. For example, consider the workers who assemble a high tech medical device that separates blood products. They may already gain a great deal of professional satisfaction simply from doing a complex job well. However, think of the additional level of job satisfaction those who value their social lens might obtain if they were able to see testimonials from patients whose lives were saved as a result of this technology. When you can help people who value their social lens see the connections between your idea and the social contribution of their work, they will be more likely to volunteer that extra 20% of engagement—if not for you, then for the society to which they want to contribute.

SOCIETY LENS: EXAMPLE 1

People who work in the fast food industry are plagued with the negative commentary of its detractors. The term "hamburger flipper," used with disdain by comedians and newscasters to indicate someone with a next-to-worthless job, is particularly repugnant to them. In 2003, the term "McJob" was added to Merriam-Webster's Collegiate Dictionary, defined as "a low-paying job that requires little skill and provides little opportunity for advancement." Jim Cantalupo, former CEO of McDonald's, called this "a slap in the face" to all restaurant employees.

Fred was a long-term employee of a fast food restaurant chain who viewed the counter and grill personnel through his Society Lens. Although he had done time in the penitentiary as a young man, his company took a chance on him when he got out. It hired him to work the counter and, later, to cook the product. He rose through the ranks to become a senior executive whose responsibilities included helping others who had stepped onto the wrong side of the law make the transition back to society. Whereas some may see his company as a fast food machine, he saw it as an opportunity for young people to learn responsibility and perhaps get a start on a career. Fred viewed his company through his Society Lens and, for that reason, dedicated his professional life to the organization. Although the turnover rate of counter and grill personnel is extremely high in this business, I know managers and executives who truly believe their primary role is to grow young people. Because they view their job through their societal lens, they are able to help young people recognize they are more than hamburger flippers and to encourage them to stay around long enough to advance their careers. For these managers, it is not about the hamburger.

Fred's motivation is rooted in his concern for his employees and the opportunity he can provide them to step out on a new path. John, in the following example, draws satisfaction from his firm's impact on the health and safety of his customers' employees.

SOCIETY LENS: EXAMPLE 2

John is a leading expert in his area of plant safety, and is committed to the idea of Saving Lives. He is able to attract top young talent to his firm because of its reputation and the technical experience they will gain. However, one of the things that holds them there is John's absolute passion for keeping people safe in the workplace. While his monthly status reports to his employees are sometimes a bit dull, his passion lights up his face, and the room, when he reports to them what he sees through his own Society Lens. When John tells his employees how their work has enabled plant workers to return alive and unhurt to their families, his passion is contagious. John helps his people view their organization through that same lens, and this imbues any idea he presents with an aura of social significance.

It is well worth providing any information that will enable employees to see the relationship between your idea and its positive impact on the larger world, as seen through their Society Lens. The quick-service restaurant example shows that it is not simply enough to recognize that people value their social lens, but to help them connect the dots between your ideas and an impact they feel is socially significant. In the case of John and his passion for plant safety, it's easy for his employees to connect his ideas to that social good, because he lives and breathes for that connection. This example also makes clear the necessity of ensuring that the contribution is genuine. If a leader mouths words about a company's impact on society but doesn't truly believe them, people will quickly see the hypocrisy.

The implications of these two examples for you as a leader are 1) You need to be clear on what you see through your own social lens and the degree to which you truly care; 2) You need to be convinced that the relationship you claim between your idea and a positive social impact is fact-based and valid; and, 3) You need to deliver the idea through your actions as well as your words.

YOUR TURN

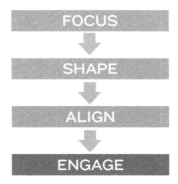

Step 4:
Engage Your Idea for Commitment

This section guides you through a process of Engaging the Idea you identified at the beginning of the chapter. It includes:

DESCRIBE THE ENGAGEMENT OF YOUR IDEA.

CONDUCT A SUCCESS FACTOR ANALYSIS OF YOUR IDEA.

CONDUCT A RISK FACTOR ANALYSIS OF YOUR IDEA.

IDENTIFY SPECIFIC ACTIONS TO STRENGTHEN THE ENGAGEMENT OF YOUR IDEA.

Describe The Current Level Of Engagement Of Your Idea

WHAT ARE YOU THINKING?

Before you conduct your Success Factor and Risk Factor Analyses on the following pages, take a moment to describe the current Engagement of your idea with three employees or other stakeholders.

EXERCISE

1. List several individuals who represent distinct employee or stakeholder groups who you need to engage with your idea.

2. Identify with an 'X' the 1-2 lenses each person is likely to consider most important when evaluating your idea.

3. Indicate WIFM ("What's in it for me?") for each person to accept and act on your idea as you would like him to.

Helpful Hint: It is better to start with only three representative employees or other stakeholders—you can always extend the list later. Try to select them, for the purpose of this exercise, so that they represent a diversity of perspectives of people who will be important to making your idea a success in the long run. For example, you might consider a high-level executive, a mid-manager and a front-line worker; or you might consider using different generational groups or people from different geographic regions.

EXERCISE

REPRESENTATIVE EMPLOYEES OR OTHER STAKEHOLDERS	PROFESSIONAL VALUES	TEAM	ORGANIZATION	PERSONAL VALUES	FAMILY	SOCIETY
PERSON #1:						
WIFM:						
PERSON #2:						
WIFM:						
PERSON #3:						
WIFM:						

Success Factor Analysis: Engagement

The following pages describe five Success Factors related to Engagement. The underlying principle of all five can be expressed in the adage, "You can bring a horse to water, but you can't make it drink." In the language of this book, that could be rephrased as "You can deliver an idea to an organization, but you can't force anyone to accept that delivery."

SUCCESS FACTORS RELATED TO ENGAGEMENT

4.1 Evidence-based validity

4.2 Trust-based credibility

4.3 Pride of participation

4.4 Empowerment

4.5 Commitment to the idea

The benefits of ensuring these Engagement-related Success Factors are in place include the following:

- You will be in a better position to predict who will accept your idea, and why, and how to increase the acceptance level among a broader range of constituents.

- You will be able to more quickly transfer the momentum of an idea developed during the process of the initiative to the people who you wish to act on it when it is delivered to the organization.

- Employees and other stakeholders will be more likely to volunteer that extra 20% of themselves that can make the difference between apathy and engaged support.

As you review the Engagement-related Success Factors in the following pages, consider how you can use them to increase the acceptance rate of the idea you described on the previous page.

EVIDENCE-BASED VALIDITY

An idea has evidence-based validity if it can be shown to be rooted in hard facts. This is a necessary criterion of acceptance for stakeholders who view an idea through their professional lenses of science or logic. Unfortunately, the ideas forwarded by many initiatives are based on no more than hunches and good intentions. When an idea is based on the physical sciences, the rules of validity are well-established in accepted practices for research design and testing. When the idea is based on social science principles such as those used in psychology, marketing or organizational dynamics, there is more room for debate. The validity of such ideas is harder to demonstrate because controlled research is not possible and the logic of the analysis may be dependent on the particular school of thought held by any one professional in the field. This is why many ideas delivered through even large scale initiatives are not based on any real evidence of their validity, but simply reflect the knowledge and experience—and sometimes the hopes and dreams—of long-time practitioners.

If significant organizational resources are to be invested in an idea, that idea should be subjected to rigorous analysis. Even if hard data is not available, the proponent of such an idea should be required to lay out a logical argument to defend its validity. If hard evidence is not available, then the unproven supporting assumptions need to be specified and also defended.

This sort of analysis of an idea is the responsibility of a leader who chooses to move an idea forward through an organizational initiative. Critical review by peers and stake-holders will result in a more finely-tuned idea with a higher likelihood of success—or, it may reveal the idea is critically flawed. It is interesting to note that while a million-dollar project in science and engineering takes such analysis for granted, equivalent amounts are invested in softer but equally important ideas with no such analysis. Fewer initiatives would fail if more effort were given to the validation of the ideas they are intended to deliver to the organization.

To what extent is this success factor in place? ☐ More than adequate
☐ Adequate
☐ Inadequate

TRUST-BASED CREDIBILITY

No matter how valid an idea is or how much hard evidence is behind it, people will not accept it if they do not find it credible as they view it through their own professional or personal lenses. For most people, trust in an idea and, especially, the person supporting it, is far more important than its evidence-based validity. One reason for this: people vote from their hearts, particularly when asked to volunteer that extra 20%. A more practical reason is that most people don't have the technical knowledge and expertise to evaluate the validity of an idea from a discipline other than their own. When a leader accepts an idea proposed by a team of experts outside of his own specialty, he accepts it on trust. While he may insist that the idea has evidence-based validity, he can only get that evidence second-hand. That is, he must trust that his experts know what they are talking about as they provide their logical analysis.

Employees almost always default to doubt when they see a new initiative coming. This is because, as noted in the opening chapter, most people expect most initiatives to have no long-term impact. If you don't see indicators of doubt, you need to look harder because they will be there. Until you uncover them, and deal with them head on, they will drag the initiative down before it begins.

This is a case where actions speak a lot louder than words. People will look for real changes in leadership behavior before they decide to commit to an initiative and the idea it delivers to the organization. At the beginning of an initiative, take some deliberate action to demonstrate that the change is real. This might be in the form of a new reward structure, moving people in or out of positions to fit the requirements of the initiative, or publicly investing financial or political capital on behalf of the initiative. Recognize that the credibility of an initiative—and the credibility of the idea it delivers—depends primarily on the credibility of the leader who backs it.

To what extent is this success factor in place?

☐ More than adequate
☐ Adequate
☐ Inadequate

PRIDE OF PARTICIPATION

Pride of participation means that an employee has viewed an idea through his own lens and personally identifies with it. When that happens, he will care what happens to the idea and will provide support when it is required. An employee who enjoys telling friends about working for a well-respected company takes pride in the company. This pride is not in the bricks and mortar, but in the idea the company represents for its employees—its employer brand.

The same is true when an employee decides to support an initiative. Once he invests himself in the idea the initiative is to deliver, pride of participation becomes a self-fulfilling prophesy. Pride attracts others who then also take ownership and become proud of their participation. Thus, the first step to fostering pride in an idea promoted by an initiative is to demonstrate pride in it yourself. When the pride of participants first begins to glow in response, early in the initiative process, nurture it into a flame that will attract the attention of others. Publicly recognize early contributions of employees and other stakeholders so that others see the opportunity for their participation to be acknowledged. Doing this on the occasion of reaching significant milestones is useful, but it is more important to integrate recognition into daily interactions with employees and their managers.

People probably won't explicitly tell you they are proud of their participation, so you need to monitor it in other ways, primarily through one-on-one conversations. Watch employees' non-verbal communications as you talk with them about the initiative. Do their eyes light up when they talk about it? Are they enjoying telling you about their role? Does their excitement attract the interest of others? Is their personal momentum in support of the initiative on the increase? If so, you are on the right track. If not, consider it an indication of an emerging vulnerability of the idea you are delivering to the organization.

To what extent is this success factor in place?   □ More than adequate
                                                 □ Adequate
                                                 □ Inadequate

EMPOWERMENT

Empowerment means enabling others to take ownership of your idea and to make independent decisions about it. This is difficult for a leader to do when she is launching her pet idea, the one in which she has invested her reputation and other professional and personal resources. Nevertheless, you can't both deliver a package and hang on to it; nor can you expect others to take ownership of your idea if you aren't willing to give up a bit of ownership yourself.

Empowerment is a balancing act in which a leader must juggle four separate components of empowerment: shared purpose, autonomy, limits and support.

Shared purpose, as discussed in chapter 1, ensures that individuals to which the idea is delivered are aligned with the anticipated short- and long-term outcomes of the idea. Autonomy refers to the freedom individuals have to choose the methods they will use to achieve the results expected of them. Limits defines the boundaries within which individuals must operate when they make those choices—an effective leader steps in only when these clearly defined limits are transgressed. Finally, support refers to the resources individuals need to achieve results including intangibles such as expertise, mentoring and political capital as well as tangibles such as budget, equipment or space.

One reason initiatives fail is that leaders hand them over to an initiative team and give them little additional thought—an act of abdication rather than empowerment. Another is that they hang on to them so tightly that the best and the brightest in the organization don't see anything to gain, as they view it through their own personal lenses, and take no interest in it. Juggling the components of empowerment is a skill anyone who leads through ideas needs to master.

To what extent is this success factor in place?

☐ More than adequate
☐ Adequate
☐ Inadequate

COMMITMENT TO THE IDEA

Commitment to an idea means that an employee, when given a choice, will commit personal resources, primarily time and energy, to supporting and moving it forward over some other set of ideas. The reality is that employees have a wide choice of ideas, both personal and professional, in which they can invest themselves—so many that they cannot possibly invest themselves in them all. This is why employees have to make such choices many times every day. In fact, one of the reasons employees fail to commit themselves to an idea is not that it lacks validity or credibility, but simply that so many ideas are thrown their way that they cannot possibly seriously commit to them all.

It is relatively easy for a leader to generate some level of excitement, or at least interest, in an initiative when it is first launched. It is quite another to turn this into the long-term commitment of employees to an idea. The best way to do this is to keep in touch with the employees charged with planning and implementing the initiative as well as those who must support the idea once it is delivered to the organization. Get their input on the focus of the idea, the form in which it is presented, and the ideas with which it is aligned or not aligned. The momentum of your idea may begin with the enthusiasm of the initiative team but will be sustained by the commitment of those employees who choose to accept the idea upon delivery.

Involving people early in the initiative process has the added benefit of identifying issues that can be addressed before they become problems. As you interact with employees, you will learn how to design your communications in ways that will allow them to answer the question, "Why should I care about this idea more than all of the other ideas to which I could choose to commit that extra 20% of my personal resources of time, energy and attention?"

To what extent is this success factor in place?

- ☐ More than adequate
- ☐ Adequate
- ☐ Inadequate

Risk Factor Analysis: Engagement

The common theme of the risk factors below is that if you don't invest the time and resources required to understand the perspectives of those you wish to act on your idea, there is a strong likelihood that they will refuse to accept delivery of the idea the initiative has forwarded to them.

RISK FACTORS RELATED TO ENGAGEMENT

4.1 Doubt creep

4.2 The idea is disowned

4.3 Lost momentum

4.4 The conversation goes negative

4.5 Volunteers find other causes

Attending to these risk factors, preferably far in advance of the time the initiative actually delivers the idea to the organization, will help you to avoid the following typical types of failures.

- A well-executed initiative has a disappointing impact because the organization was not prepared to accept the idea upon delivery.
- An idea seems to be initially well accepted but, within months, it disappears with a "poof."
- People you hope will act on the idea simply don't care.

As you read the detail on each of these Engagement-related risk factors, remember that—even if you have attended to each of the Success Factors in the previous three chapters—your idea will fail to have its desired impact if it doesn't engage the hearts and minds of those you wish to act on it. That is, they will be unwilling to volunteer that 20% of time and effort that spells the difference between success and failure of your idea.

DOUBT CREEP

An initiative is dead in the water as soon as employees and other stakeholders no longer have confidence in any significant aspect of it: They suspect the assumptions on which it is based are faulty, they don't think the purpose it is supposed to serve is legitimate, they don't believe the implementation plan is practical, or, most lethal of all, they don't believe their leadership is committed. Once credibility falters, the question of "why bother" begins to seep through the psyche of those required to carry out the initiative and support the idea it delivers to the organization.

Once credibility is lost, a domino effect begins and it is very difficult to regain—starting with lessened commitment and ending with abandonment of support for the idea. This is why credibility must be monitored and nurtured from the start of the initiative through to the acceptance of the idea by the people of the organization and their ongoing support of it.

RISK INDICATORS

- ☐ Employees ask questions or make wry comments that suggest misgivings about the initiative.
- ☐ People make no preparations for changes in their own plans or behaviors that accepting and acting on the idea would require.
- ☐ Owners of functions or processes that would be affected by the idea take no action to accommodate those changes.
- ☐ Ground level budgets and plans for the following year do not reflect an expectation of change as a result of the initiative.
- ☐ People hold off committing to the initiative until they know for sure that it "is real."

How important is this risk to your idea?

- ☐ Not important
- ☐ Important
- ☐ Critical

RISK MITIGATION: SEE SUCCESS FACTORS 4.1 & 4.2.

THE IDEA IS DISOWNED

Employees engage with an idea and volunteer that extra 20% because, when they believe the cause to be important, they feel important. When they are proud of the idea promoted by an initiative, they feel proud of themselves and they take personal ownership of the idea.

As a leader, you can never discount pride as a significant motivator. When your people no longer see what originally got them engaged, their pride in the idea—and their commitment to it—will begin to fade. Consequently, their sense of ownership also fades until, finally, the idea is disowned. When this happens, they may need help in regaining that perspective that originally attracted them to the idea, or in finding meaning through another one of their lenses.

RISK INDICATORS

- ☐ People no longer brag to others about the initiative with which they are involved or the idea it is delivering to the organization.

- ☐ People distance themselves from the idea before or after it is delivered to the organization.

- ☐ People talk about their involvement with an initiative as an obligation rather than an opportunity.

- ☐ When asked what they have been doing, employees make no mention of the initiative, the idea it is promoting, or its impact on their own work.

How important is this risk to your idea?   ☐ Not important
                                                  ☐ Important
                                                  ☐ Critical

RISK MITIGATION: SEE SUCCESS FACTORS 4.3 & 4.5.

LOST MOMENTUM

Enthusiasm and commitment are contagious within a team. So are apathy and indifference. When one member no longer finds the initiative meaningful, others may soon follow. This can be disastrous when the majority of the team finds its value through the same lens. For example, when a team of engineers no longer believes that the initiative is based on sound science—or, a sales team feels an idea with which their customers disagree is being forced upon them.

A successful initiative team acquires a life of its own that both nourishes and feeds on the idea it promotes. When the vitality of the team fades, so does the vitality of the idea. Although it may be difficult to measure this vitality, it is very easy to feel— which is why it is important for leaders to attend team meetings and otherwise keep in personal touch with initiative participants.

RISK INDICATORS

☐ Employees no longer even bother to express doubts about the initiative, simply dismissing it as not worth their attention.

☐ People show up late for team meetings, or miss them.

☐ People do not linger and talk after team meetings.

☐ Key personnel send substitutes to meetings.

☐ Team morale is on the decline.

How important is this risk to your idea?

☐ Not important
☐ Important
☐ Critical

RISK MITIGATION: SEE SUCCESS FACTORS 4.3, 4.4 & 4.5.

THE CONVERSATION GOES NEGATIVE

When people no longer feel an idea being promoted by an initiative is going to be successful, they may seek to protect their own self-image as well as their careers by looking for people or conditions to blame, rather than acknowledging their own roles or what they might do to help the situation. At this point, speaking negatively becomes a mutually reinforcing team sport, distracting each other's attention from the tough questions.

There is virtually no hope for an idea if the atmosphere has turned negative because the negativity has probably already spread beyond the initiative team to the broader group of stakeholders and others whose support will be needed for success.

RISK INDICATORS

☐ Subtle, and not so subtle, sarcasm enters into conversation.

☐ There are more complaints raised than solutions offered.

☐ A lot of finger-pointing occurs.

☐ The room goes silent when the initiative's leader walks in.

How important is this risk to your idea?

☐ Not important
☐ Important
☐ Critical

RISK MITIGATION: SEE SUCCESS FACTORS 4.2 & 4.3.

VOLUNTEERS FIND OTHER CAUSES

Always remember that the success of your initiative, and the idea it delivers to the organization, is dependent on how your people are directing that 20% of volunteered effort—the effort they give because they are engaged with your organization and your ideas. When the idea promoted by your initiative is no longer engaging, people will decline to volunteer this important 20%, and they may give less and less of the remaining 80%. People's abandonment of an idea in favor of ideas more personally meaningful to them is the ultimate result of the loss of its credibility, the loss of personal pride people take in it, the loss of team momentum, and the negative perspectives that follow.

RISK INDICATORS

- ☐ People do only what is necessary to meet expectations.
- ☐ The best people get themselves assigned to other projects.
- ☐ People no longer ask to be on the project.
- ☐ Those who were excited to get the initiative started are not excited about implementing it.

How important is this risk to your idea?

- ☐ Not important
- ☐ Important
- ☐ Critical

RISK MITIGATION: SEE SUCCESS FACTORS 4.3, 4.4 & 4.5.

.

Thought-Provoking Questions About The Engagement Of Ideas

You will find that it is easier to think about the risks addressed in this chapter, and to help others think about them, by asking questions. Use the following questions to inquire about one or more of the ideas you have considered in this chapter.

- Who do you need to be committed to this idea for it to have the impact you need? What's in it for them?
- Why should people care who:
  - Are strongly committed to this organization? [Organizational lens]
  - Are on teams whose support you need? [Team lens]
  - Will evaluate this idea in terms of their professional expertise? [Professional lens]
- How will people whose commitment you need view this idea from the perspective of:
  - Their personal beliefs and values? [Beliefs and Values lens]
  - The welfare of their families? [Family lens]
  - The impact of the initiative on society? [Societal lens]

NOW WHAT?

Review your assessment of the Success Factors and Risk Factors and indicate what actions, if any, are required to increase the effectiveness of your idea.

PART II

EXTENDING THE FOUR-STEP METHOD BEYOND ORGANIZATIONAL INITIATIVES

BEYOND ORGANIZATIONAL INITIATIVES

You now recognize that the approach I call "Leading Through Ideas" applies to more than organizational initiatives—you have frequently seen examples of ideas delivered through other processes: meetings in which ideas get ignored, projects in which ideas get sidetracked, mergers in which ideas get confused, sales presentations in which ideas get rejected, sticky notes that hang ideas on cash registers, a presentation to the board by an R&D group and many others.

Now, I'd like you to think about two ideas that are critical to your success: 1) The idea of The-Organization-You-Lead; and, 2) The idea of Yourself-as-Leader. If you are like most leaders, you probably have never thought of these as individual ideas that are critical to your organization and leadership, let alone carefully analyzed how you present them to your organization. However, the way in which your employees, colleagues, bosses and other stakeholders view these two ideas subtly influences how they respond to your leadership practices and everything else that happens in your organization. Arguably, the most important work you can do as an idea leader is to apply the principles of focus, shape, alignment and engagement to these two ideas.

In each of the following two chapters, you will be able to follow along with two leaders as they go through this process: the first dealing with the idea of his organization, and the second the idea of herself. At each step of the way, you will have the opportunity to apply the same process to your own situation. When you do this, you will find that the principles you learned in the context of organizational initiatives apply equally well to these two important ideas.

The brief final chapter in this section, "Balancing Tensions Among Ideas," focuses on the common situation where key ideas are in conflict with each other. For this purpose, I will return to the case study of the Arthur Andersen partnership as an object lesson. I will ask you to stand back and take a realistic look at the balancing act you inevitably face as you simultaneously manage multiple and sometimes conflicting ideas among constituents with divergent perspectives.

CHAPTER 5
The Idea of
The-Organization-You-Lead

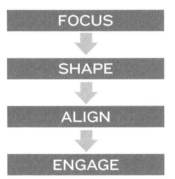

FOCUS

SHAPE

ALIGN

ENGAGE

THE IDEA OF
THE ORGANIZATION YOU LEAD
IN A NUTSHELL

Your role as a leader is to develop and nurture the idea of The-Organization-You-Lead, maintaining its Focus, Shape, Alignment and Engagement to ensure maximum momentum and impact.

KEY POINTS

The idea of The-Organization-You-Lead is subject to the same principles that apply to ideas delivered by organizational initiatives and other processes.

> **Focusing** the idea of The-Organization-You-Lead will avoid unnecessary diffusion of time, money and political capital by targeting people's actions on its purpose.
>
> **Shaping** the idea of The-Organization-You-Lead will enable people to pick it up, carry it forward, and hand it off to others, increasing the likelihood that it will achieve its purpose.
>
> **Aligning** the idea of The-Organization-You-Lead so that people can see its relevance to other energized ideas will increase its momentum.
>
> **Engaging** the idea of The-Organization-You-Lead allows people to see the relationship between it and the ideas they hold of themselves, giving them the motivation to go the extra mile in support of it.

Case Study: Observe how the CEO of Acme Manufacturing analyzes and refines the idea of his organization as part of a culture change initiative after a merger of separate business units.

Exercise: You may assess and develop the idea of The-Organization-You-Lead as you follow along with the Acme case study.

A SAMPLE OF STATEMENTS ABOUT VISION, MISSION AND VALUES

VISION

ALBERTSONS:
To be known as the favorite neighborhood food and drug retailer in every market where we do business, with helpful associates, competitive prices and high quality, fresh products.

COLGATE:
Colgate's vision is to become the best truly global products company.

STARBUCKS:
From the beginning, our vision at Starbucks has been to create a "third place" between home and work where people can come together to enjoy the peace and pleasure of coffee and community.

MISSION

GOOGLE:
Google's mission is to organize the world's information and make it universally accessible and useful.

GILLETTE:
Gillette has been at the heart of men's grooming for over 100 years. Each day, more than 800 million men around the world trust their faces and skin to Gillette's innovative razors and shaving products. This commitment to giving men the very best is carried into our line of personal care products, including deodorant and body wash. All designed for the unique needs of men – helping them to look, feel and be their best every day.

WALGREENS:
To be the most trusted, convenient multichannel provider and advisor of innovative pharmacy, health and wellness solutions, and consumer goods and services in communities across America. A destination where health and happiness come together to help people get well, stay well and live well.

VALUES

Values statements range from a very few words to a few pages. Following is a very short but representative sample of values explicitly listed on just a few of the above corporate websites: can-do attitude, caring, commitment, community, compassionate, continuous improvement, corporate citizenship, courage, driven, emotional resilience, fun, honesty, initiative, integrity, quality, safety, sustainability, teamwork, and trust.

NOTE:
All of the above were explicitly described as Vision, Mission or Values on the respective corporate websites.

HOW DO OTHERS THINK ABOUT YOUR ORGANIZATION?

What is the first thing that comes to an employee's mind when she is about to tell a family member, a friend or a customer about your organization? If the answer to this question is important to you, you will want to think about how you have presented the idea of The-Organization-You-Lead to your employees and to your many other constituents.

Whether you are conscious of it or not, you present the idea of The-Organization-You-Lead on a daily basis in a wide variety of settings and formats. Therefore, one of your most important responsibilities as a leader is to develop and nurture your basic idea of your organization itself. Because you may want different people to act in different ways and even for different purposes, the idea of the organization may take on a variety of forms. For example, most corporate websites will express the idea of the organization under titles such as "Future Vision," "Mission Statement," or "Core Values". Sometimes you will deliver the idea of your organization less formally, as when you introduce your organization over lunch to partners, customers, vendors or other collaborators. You will use other approaches when you deliver the idea of The-Organization-You-Lead to analysts, key investors or board members, and still others when you share it with employees and even family members.

You will lead more effectively if you create consistency in your message and take account of who receives that message. No matter what approach you use to deliver the idea of The-Organization-You-Lead, you must be aware that how you choose to Shape that idea, Align it with other ideas, and position it for Engagement will depend on who you want to act on it, how they will act, and for what purpose. The time you take to do this will undoubtedly pay off in the increased efficiency with which the organization achieves its purpose because of a tighter Focus, a more effective Shape, more efficient Alignment and, especially, a higher level of Engagement with the members of your team and their employees.

The remainder of this chapter will describe how you can craft the idea of The-Organization-You-Lead—to take charge of how your stakeholders envision it and, especially, act on it. Note that these are the same steps you followed when developing ideas delivered by organizational initiatives. The difference is simply one of breadth. Ideally, all of the ideas within your organization should be consistent with the idea of the organization. While it is impossible to achieve this goal completely, it will point you in the right direction.

STEP I: FOCUS THE IDEA OF THE-ORGANIZATION-YOU-LEAD
First, identify the Purpose you wish to achieve by delivering the idea of The-Organization-You-Lead to your employees and other constituents—this will help you to answer the critical question, "Why am I spending my limited time and energy, and that of my people, on moving this idea forward?" Second, define Who you want to take What Actions as a result of accepting delivery of the idea of The-Organization-You-Lead.

STEP 2: SHAPE THE IDEA OF THE-ORGANIZATION-YOU-LEAD

Mold the idea of The-Organization-You-Lead into the shape that will enable people to pick it up, carry it forward, and hand it off to others. This will increase the likelihood that they will use it to achieve its intended purpose with a minimum of distraction or confusion.

STEP 3: ALIGN THE IDEA OF THE-ORGANIZATION-YOU-LEAD

Scan the organization for aligned and non-aligned ideas that may help or hinder the idea of The-Organization-You-Lead. This will enable you to leverage the energy that already exists in the organization. It will also avoid having it dragged down or off course by ideas that are counter-productive to your intentions.

STEP 4: ENGAGE THE IDEA OF THE-ORGANIZATION-YOU-LEAD

Look at your idea through the lenses of others so you can anticipate the primary question each will consciously or unconsciously ask about your idea, "What's in it for me?" Enabling people to see the relationship between the idea of the organization with the ideas they hold of themselves—who they are now, what they value and what they want to become—will help them give that extra 20% that will differentiate your organization from its competition.

As you try out each of these steps yourself, you will be able to refer to the case study of the CEO of Acme Manufacturing as he analyzes and refines the idea of his organization.

Prior To Step 1:
Put Your Stake In The Ground

Start to think about the idea of The-Organization-You-Lead by putting some boundaries around it, clarifying in your own mind what you do and don't want it to represent. I encourage you to use only a few words or a short phrase, as if your organization were a can of peas and you needed to put a label on it. This level of specificity will put you on the right track for turning a general intention into an idea with a purpose.

The name you create now may be the name by which you and others refer to the idea of The-Organization-You-Lead as you work your way through the entire process, but don't be surprised if you decide to change it along the way. Some of these steps, particularly the first one, operate on the chicken-or-egg principle—you can't define one until you have defined the other. You might start with a generic name such as mission, vision or values, or a phrase such as "Who we are," or "What we believe," or "The [company name] Way." You could choose to narrow its focus to something like "Quality at [company name]," or you might choose a name that is context-specific, such as, "Our [new product] is the foundation of our future," or "We take ownership of our mistakes." At this step of the process, the most important thing is to be sure the name of the idea of The-Organization-You-Lead carries the connotations you want it to. This is the first step in branding your idea, i.e., of establishing a presence in the marketplace of ideas.

WHAT THE CEO DID

The following example will demonstrate how the CEO of Acme Manufacturing approached this task.

ACME MANUFACTURING: BACKGROUND

The new CEO of a $100M company, Acme Manufacturing, recently merged three different business units into a single organization. The largest of these had been troubled with poor morale, poor quality and low customer satisfaction. Having moved the entire operation into a brand new facility, the CEO saw this as an opportunity to clarify and strengthen the idea of Acme Manufacturing for himself, his executive team and, ultimately, for each of his 700 employees.

To put some initial boundaries around this idea, the CEO gave a name to it and identified the processes by which it would be delivered:

WHAT DO YOU NAME THIS IDEA? The New Acme

WHAT ARE THE PROCESSES BY WHICH THIS IDEA WILL BE DELIVERED TO THE ORGANIZATION?
Initial meetings with my executive team, their meetings with their direct reports and so on, cascaded to hourly workers. Also frequent brief, informal one-on-one interactions between everyone who has direct reports and their employees.

WHAT THE CEO WAS THINKING

Naming the idea was simple. The CEO slightly modified the formal name of his organization with the adjective "new" to remind himself that he was talking about a company that would have a culture quite different from the old.

Deciding on the processes by which the idea would be delivered was more difficult. He could think of literally hundreds of ways his idea would be carried to the organization. He also knew that he wanted his employees to see the idea of The New Acme implicit in everything he and his executive team did or said. However, to keep his thinking focused, he decided to concentrate on one formal approach (a series of cascaded meetings) and one informal (frequent, brief one-on-one interactions). He expected the informal process to have the greatest overall impact.

WHAT ARE YOU THINKING?

Now, identify the name to which you will refer to the idea of The-Organization-You-Lead throughout this exercise. It may simply be the name of your company, but it is often better to use a word or phrase that reflects a characteristic you would like to emphasize. Note that you may wish to fine-tune your response to the following two questions as you move through the other steps of this exercise.

EXERCISE

What do you name this idea (the idea of The-Organization-You-Lead)?

What are the processes by which this idea will delivered to the organization? (Limit to a maximum of 3)

Step 1:
Focus The Idea Of
The-Organization-You-Lead

Now you are ready to focus the idea of The-Organization-You-Lead. As you recall from Chapter 1, this involves clarifying the purpose, actors and actions associated with this idea.

It is easiest to approach this step in two segments:

      1-A: Identify the Purpose of the idea of The-Organization-You-Lead

      1-B: Identify the Actors and Actions

Purpose is the most essential of the three components when focusing the idea of The-Organization-You-Lead—if you don't know why it is important to deliver the idea, then it is impossible to decide how to make decisions about who you want to take action on it or what actions you want them to take. No matter how you define the idea of your organization, whether on the back of a napkin or through a million dollar process run by consultants, you still have to focus that idea by asking yourself: "Who do I want to take what actions in response to the idea of The-Organization-I-Lead, and for what purpose?"

Step 1-A:
Identify the Purpose of the Idea of
The-Organization-You-Lead

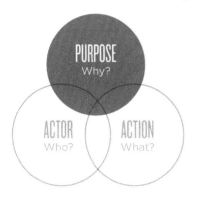

Most organizations have a description of their purpose written down somewhere. Sometimes it is labeled as a purpose statement, and other times it is embedded in statements about mission, vision and/or values as shown earlier in this chapter. You will find these statements in corporate brochures, annual reports and websites. Sometimes they will be engraved on a plaque in the lobby. Unfortunately, in more than a few of these organizations, even the top executives only vaguely recall these purpose statements several months after they have been written. I once coached a senior executive who, one month after his team spent a day creating a list of the six points of their mission statement, held up a twenty-dollar bill and said he would give it to anyone on his team who could specify all six—and he got to keep his twenty dollars.

The executives in that situation actually took their mission, vision and values quite seriously as they discussed their plans with their peers and as they communicated formally and informally with their employees. Nevertheless, even with that level of commitment, no one could remember all six points. I cite it here to illustrate the challenge of turning such purpose statements into meaningful actions. The lesson here: The better articulated these statements are, and the more frequently they are demonstrated in actions as well as words, the more likely it is that ideas throughout the organization will be focused on a common purpose. Also keep in mind that the further removed from the executive suite an individual employee is, the more important it is to expend the resources necessary for that employee to see the relationship between the matters he deals with on a daily basis and the larger purpose of the organization.

WHAT THE CEO DID

The following case example describes how the CEO of Acme Manufacturing defined the purpose of the idea of The New Acme.

THE PURPOSE OF THE IDEA OF THE NEW ACME

LONG-TERM PURPOSE:

Achieve a unified and committed belief among employees that we do whatever it takes to meet the needs of our customers, a belief that will be demonstrated in their behaviors at all levels. The idea that we are, first and foremost, a customer-centric organization is an idea that is here to stay.

DESIRED SHORT-TERM IMPACT:

Employee commitment to quality, as defined by each work team, will increase; employee morale also will improve, as measured by survey scores; customers will begin to recognize that we are committed to improving the quality of the product and services we deliver to them.

WHAT THE CEO WAS THINKING

The CEO actually knew a lot of ways he wanted his organization to change, ranging from a more efficient supply chain to the sales force keeping in closer touch with its customers. He was actively working on many of them, but, he wanted to focus on something with which everyone in the organization could identify and that could be expressed in measurable terms. In addition, both the immediate impact and the long-term purpose dealt directly with one of Acme's most pressing issues: decreasing customer satisfaction. THE CEO also believed that achieving these purposes would give him a leg up on solving many of the other issues he was facing such as his supply chain and customer intimacy concerns.

WHAT ARE YOU THINKING?

Now, identify the short-term impact and the long-term purpose of the idea you are going to deliver to The-Organization-You-Lead, i.e., the idea of the organization itself. Remember, keeping it simple will help you to identify your highest priorities.

EXERCISE

What is the long-term purpose of the idea you named at the beginning of this exercise? (Limit to one)

What are the short-term objectives of this idea? (Maximum of three)

Step 1-B:
Define Who You Want To Take What Actions In Response To Your Idea

The challenge of this part of the focusing process is to narrow down the actor and actions to a very small number. In reality, of course, you will want every one of your employees and other stakeholders to take many actions in response to your idea. However, identifying a small number at the outset will force you and your team to get quite clear and concrete about how the idea of The-Organization-You-Lead will be transformed into reality by individual people taking specific actions. If you and your team cannot clearly articulate this new idea and why it is important, the rest of the organization certainly will not be able to do so.

Clarifying the who and the what will also help you further specify exactly what the purpose of your idea is. Finally, it will give you a stronger foundation on which to consider issues of Shape, Alignment and Engagement in subsequent steps. You will eventually expand the list of both actors and actions, but it is better to start small.

WHAT THE CEO DID

The CEO of Acme focused the who and what of his idea by identifying the representative actors and actions desired in response to the idea of The New Acme.

REPRESENTATIVE ACTOR	ACTION
PERSON #1: The employee who makes arrangements with the shipping company for express deliveries.	If she spots anything that seems out of order or may interfere with customer satisfaction, she will take action to remedy the situation, even if it is not within her normal job responsibilities to do so.
PERSON #2: The inside sales rep who takes an order for parts or supplies.	When a customer requests an item other than what that customer usually orders, the rep will ask specific questions to ensure the item is appropriate to the application and to identify related items or information the customer may not realize she needs.
PERSON #3: The front line supervisor of an employee who assembles parts.	The supervisor will meet weekly with his team to reinforce the idea of The New Acme so that they can describe what it is and how it translates into their job activities and to overall company success.

WHAT THE CEO WAS THINKING

At this point, it wasn't only the CEO who was thinking, because he had wisely involved his direct reports and some of their team members in the discussion. He did this to sharpen his own thinking but, more important, to allow those who needed to accept the idea to take ownership of it themselves.

The biggest challenge the CEO faced in getting his team on board was in encouraging them to get extremely specific about who was expected to do what as a result of the idea. The tendency of most people is to talk about employees and actions in general, in order to cover all possible situations. He short-circuited this tendency by repeatedly asking his team members to give very explicit examples. He then asked for specifics: "Why are these proposed solutions the best ways to bring the idea of The New Acme to life?"

These discussions also helped them to clarify among themselves the purpose of the idea of The New Acme so that they could go back and tighten up their description of both long- and short-term results.

WHAT ARE YOU THINKING?

Now, complete the same activity for the idea of The-Organization-You-Lead—the idea you named at the beginning of this exercise. Remember that your goal is to identify three specific, representative actors and actions that best demonstrate how the purpose of your idea can be achieved. The more specific you can be now, the easier it will be for others to identify additional specific actors and actions.

EXERCISE

Identify three representative employees or stakeholders and indicate one specific action you will want each to take upon accepting the idea of The-Organization-You-Lead and integrating it into their work.

REPRESENTATIVE ACTOR	ACTION
PERSON #1:	
PERSON #2:	
PERSON #3:	

SUMMARY OF FOCUSING THE IDEA OF THE-ORGANIZATION-YOU-LEAD

Accepting the discipline of focusing the idea of The-Organization-You-Lead in this way helps you to maintain consistency of your thought and actions as well as those of others. This requires bringing the idea into day-to-day discussions of business issues and options as a basis for decision making, from the level of your executive team down to front line workers. Without this discipline, it is easy for ideas to wander off in their own directions or to become so general that they become meaningless.

Your role as a leader is to maintain the focus of The-Organization-You-Lead even when it weathers inevitable turbulent times. Your goal is to have the idea of your organization emerge from those times with a minimum of dispersed Momentum, a maximum of Alignment and with Focus intact.

Step 2:
Shape The Idea Of
The-Organization-You-Lead

Recall that the choices you make when you shape an idea affects the ease with which people can pick it up, engage with it and share it with others. Depending on how you deliver the idea of The-Organization-You-Lead, an individual will perceive it as being relatively precise or fuzzy, and relatively simple or complex. The diagram below illustrates the extremes of these dimensions. For example, the formal statements of corporate vision and, to a lesser extent, mission, tend to be relatively simple and precise, i.e., they present the idea of the company as a pointed idea. At the same time, the idea of the organization as delivered through its annual report tends to be a schematic idea, one with a high degree of complexity and a fair degree of precision. Within the website or the annual report, you will also find pages that deliver the idea of the company in simple and fuzzy terms—as a cloudy idea—usually when addressing "soft" topics such as social consciousness, care of the environment or care for its people. The idea of the company itself is rarely presented as one that is fuzzy and complex, i.e., as a turbulent idea—although its business environment may be portrayed as such.

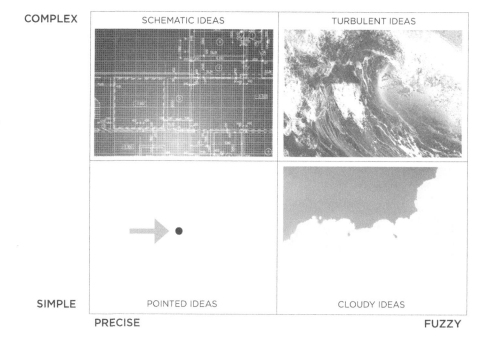

COMPLEX   SCHEMATIC IDEAS   TURBULENT IDEAS

SIMPLE   POINTED IDEAS   CLOUDY IDEAS

PRECISE   FUZZY

In Step 1, the CEO forced his team members to describe the Purpose of the idea of The New Acme as well as the simple and precise actions to be taken by representative individuals in specific situations. At that stage of his discussion, pushing his team to define the idea of The New Acme in very pointed terms forced them to move it from a relatively cloudy form of "We need to increase customer satisfaction" to specific, pointed changes. This was important because it forced them to focus their discussions and define exactly what they meant by that initially cloudy idea.

Next it was time to begin to introduce the idea of The New Acme to managers and supervisors. The CEO asked each of his direct reports to work with their teams to create a plan for delivering the idea to the broader employee base within their respective business units. They chose to do so through a 15-minute presentation at the regularly scheduled meetings of each front-line work group in the company, and its supervisor. To ensure simplicity and precision, each member of the communication team used the same PowerPoint presentations, and to ensure group involvement, they saved five minutes of each presentation for Q&A.

Unfortunately, the initial presentations did not achieve the intended results. For one, when it came time for Q&A, no one had any questions, not even the supervisors. They simply nodded their heads in agreement, glanced at the clock on the wall, and went back to work. As might be expected from that reaction, there were no noticeable changes in their work behaviors.

WHAT THE CEO DID

Upon investigation, which included one-on-one conversations with some of the supervisors and workers, as well as the communication team, the CEO decided there was a problem in the Shape of the idea of The New Acme as it was being delivered to the organization. To make his findings clear to his team, he focused on a single supervisor and two individual employees from different work groups, as shown in the example.

REPRESENTATIVE EMPLOYEE OR OTHER STAKEHOLDER	SHAPE OF IDEA AS CURRENTLY PERCEIVED (Circle one)	HOW SHAPE SHOULD BE MODIFIED FOR THIS INDIVIDUAL (Circle one in each column)	
THE EMPLOYEE WHO ARRANGES EXPRESS DELIVERIES	Pointed / **Cloudy** / Turbulent / Schematic	**More Precise** / Keep as-is / More Fuzzy	More Simple / **Keep as-is** / More Complex
THE INSIDE SALES REP	Pointed / **Cloudy** / Turbulent / Schematic	**More Precise** / Keep as-is / More Fuzzy	More Simple / **Keep as-is** / More Complex
FRONT LINE SUPERVISOR IN THE PLANT	Pointed / Cloudy / **Turbulent** / Schematic	**More Precise** / Keep as-is / More Fuzzy	More Simple / Keep as-is / **More Complex**

WHAT THE CEO WAS THINKING

Front line employees found it intimidating to meet with the CEO, but once he established trust, this is what he found: The new behaviors that seemed so clear and precise to the communications team came across to these employees as cloudy. In particular, front liners told him it was unclear how they were to translate the examples in the presentation into their own on-the-job behaviors. In addition, while they recognized customer satisfaction was important, they didn't see this message as any different from the dozens of other customer satisfaction messages they received over the last five years. They saw it as just another well-meaning but cloudy idea.

When THE CEO talked privately to the front-line supervisor, someone unafraid to speak her mind, he found her to be angry that yet another idea was being tossed down onto her team. Just in the previous week, she had received directives regarding a new safety initiative and a series of heavy-handed and demoralizing emails from the field services organization about unhappy customers. "Frankly," she said, "these things are distractions—I have enough to do to keep my team focused and motivated without having to lay this stuff on them as well." Obviously, from her perspective, the idea of customer satisfaction in general, and the idea of The New Acme in particular, was a turbulent idea.

When the CEO presented this information to his team, they confirmed that this was a common reaction of front-line employees and their supervisors. To address this problem, they decided on the following approach:

First, they would bring the supervisors on board with the idea by having discussions in advance to help them see it was not, "just another one of those ideas," but was part of a carefully crafted plan that was going to make a difference. In addition, they provided each supervisor with a simple template that she could use, with her employees, to identify just two or three specific behaviors that would 1) make sense to her team, and 2) make a difference in customer satisfaction. For the employees, this increased level of precision made the idea actionable. The fact that these actions came out of their own heads was, of course, a big help. For the supervisor, understanding additional detail about how this approach fit into the broader purpose of doing business in a new way gave her a greater level of confidence in the idea of The New Acme.

WHAT ARE YOU THINKING?

Now, take a close look at the idea of The-Organization-You-Lead that you described in Step 1. View it from the perspective of one or more people who you need to accept delivery of your idea, and decide if there is anything you should do to adjust its shape.

EXERCISE

Assess the Shape of your idea from the perspective of others:

a. Identify one or more representative employees or other stakeholders who you hope will take action on your idea.

b. For each person:
    - Indicate the shape of your idea as that individual currently sees it.
    - Indicate, for that person, if the idea needs to be reshaped on the simple-complex or precise-ambiguous dimensions.

EMPLOYEE OR OTHER STAKEHOLDER	SHAPE OF IDEA AS CURRENTLY PERCEIVED (Circle one)	HOW SHAPE SHOULD BE MODIFIED FOR THIS INDIVIDUAL (Circle one in each column)	
PERSON #1:	Pointed	More Precise	More Simple
	Cloudy	Keep as-is	Keep as-is
	Turbulent	More Fuzzy	More Complex
	Schematic		
PERSON #2:	Pointed	More Precise	More Simple
	Cloudy	Keep as-is	Keep as-is
	Turbulent	More Fuzzy	More Complex
	Schematic		
PERSON #3:	Pointed	More Precise	More Simple
	Cloudy	Keep as-is	Keep as-is
	Turbulent	More Fuzzy	More Complex
	Schematic		

SUMMARY OF SHAPING THE IDEA OF THE-ORGANIZATION-YOU-LEAD

Remember that precision almost always trumps fuzziness, and simplicity almost always trumps complexity. This is particularly true when you are delivering a single idea that's relevant to all levels of the organization. If you aim toward keeping the idea of The-Organization-You-Lead simple and precise, it will be more likely to survive in the midst of all of the other cloudy, turbulent and schematic ideas coursing through the organization at any one time.

Your role as a leader is to watch your people as they interact with the idea of your organization. Can they pick it up and share it with someone else? Do they remember it and actually apply it to their work? Does it attract their attention and generate enthusiasm? If not, step back and think about how you might refine it into a more useful shape.

Step 3:
Align The Idea Of
The-Organization-You-Lead

The success of the idea of The-Organization-You-Lead has a lot to do with how it is aligned with other ideas. If it represents an entirely new idea, it runs the risk of being held back or dragged down by existing ideas that may have already accumulated a lot of momentum. If this is the case, you need to pay serious attention to de-energizing these opposing ideas—or realigning them—in terms of one or more of the four facets depicted below. At the same time, if you can realign the vocabulary or structure of the idea of The-Organization-You-Lead, or adjust how it is perceived culturally, you may be able to utilize the momentum of already established ideas. The best way to approach this challenge is to scan the organization for aligned and non-aligned ideas that may help or hinder the idea of The-Organization-You-Lead.

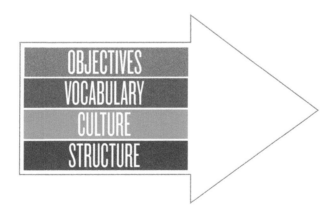

WHAT THE CEO DID

The CEO and his team actually came up with quite a few ideas floating around the organization that either supported or competed with the idea of The New Acme, but they decided four were most relevant. They listed those and rated their alignment with the idea of The New Acme. In the following example, "A" indicates an aligned idea, and "M" indicates a misaligned idea.

OTHER IDEAS IN THE ORGANIZATION THAT MAY BE RELEVANT TO YOURS	OBJECTIVES	VOCABULARY	CULTURE	STRUCTURE
BONUSES FOR PERFORMANCE - A well-established and generally appreciated component of Acme's performance management system that offered financial incentives for reaching targeted goals.	A		A	M
EMPLOYEES ARE IMPORTANT - The new CEO had already created a positive impression in this way.	A		A	
CUSTOMER COMPLAINT INDEX - This idea was promoted by a previous CEO and was viewed as both unfair and punitive.	A	M	M	M
FLAVOR-OF-THE-MONTH INITIATIVES - Even though the CEO saw his new idea as a permanent change, past experience caused most employees to doubt this.			M	

WHAT THE CEO WAS THINKING

Here is how the CEO and his team analyzed the alignment of these ideas with the new acme:

The idea of Bonuses for Performance aligned well with the idea of The New Acme since it already included the objective of customer satisfaction and reflected a culture that rewarded targeted behaviors. However, it did not align well in terms of its traditional structure, which required performance reviews only once a year, with little said about targeted behaviors in between. Thus, the CEO and his team realized that people would need to think differently about the idea of Bonuses for Performance for it to be aligned with the idea of The New Acme. This is because the new idea assumed that informal feedback occurs on a daily basis and that formal feedback be worked into monthly team meetings.

The idea that Employees are Important aligned well with the CEO's idea of The New Acme and he took every opportunity to emphasize that satisfied employees are necessary to have satisfied customers. The CEO would continue to leverage this well-received theme as he moved forward with The New Acme.

The idea of the Customer Complaint Index had been gone from the company for several years and actually had similar customer satisfaction objectives to The New Acme. However, it was totally misaligned in terms of vocabulary, as it focused on complaints rather than satisfaction. It was a poor cultural fit because it tended to view the employee as a cause of a problem rather than a potential solution, which The New Acme stressed. Finally, it misaligned in structure, since the complaint index had been an important criterion for firing people. Although the customer complaint index hadn't been used in years, it brought back sufficient bad memories that it threatened to taint the idea of The New Acme. Consequently, the CEO decided to address this issue directly as the idea was introduced, using the complaint index as a counter-example to The New Acme.

The idea of the Flavor of the Month Initiative was a strong part of the culture of Acme and acted as a drag on the idea of The New Acme. The CEO and his team recognized that the only way to detach themselves from this cultural anchor would be to create some dramatic results in the short term.

WHAT ARE YOU THINKING?

Now, go through the same process with the idea of The-Organization-You-Lead, as you have defined it in previous exercises.

EXERCISE

Assess the degree of Alignment of other ideas in the organization with your idea:

a. List other ideas in the organization that may be relevant to yours.

b. Identify the degree to which each is aligned with yours on each of the four facets of Alignment, using the following code:

- A = The idea is aligned with yours (works with your idea)
- M = The idea is misaligned with yours (works against your idea)
- Blank = neutral or uncertain

OTHER IDEAS IN THE ORGANIZATION THAT MAY BE RELEVANT TO YOURS	OBJECTIVES	VOCABULARY	CULTURE	STRUCTURE

SUMMARY OF ALIGNING THE IDEA OF THE-ORGANIZATION-YOU-LEAD

Organizations in which ideas tend to be aligned are more efficient that those in which ideas are dispersed in opposing directions. This translates into profits because resources won't be wasted by ideas pulling against each other—instead, complementary ideas will be able to build on each other. You can't personally manage the momentum of all of the ideas in your organization, nor should you even try. But you can provide a reference point in the form of a clear and compelling idea of The-Organization-You-Lead against which your employees can assess their own ideas and actions.

Your role as a leader is to ensure that this reference point is visible and that people recognize it as an idea that has your firm commitment. Then, they can be confident that it will be around for a long time. They need to believe it will be worth their time and effort to align their own ideas with the idea of The-Organization-You-Lead.

Step 4:
Engage Others With The Idea of The-Organization-You-Lead

In Chapter 4, you saw that while the first 80% of an employee's effort is given in return for salary and other benefits, the critical 20% that makes the largest difference is volunteered. It is given willingly by the employee because he finds personal meaning in the ideas that comprise the organization—in this case, the idea of The-Organization-You-Lead. You want them not only to align themselves with this idea, you want them to celebrate it. The best way to address this challenge is to look at your idea through the lenses used by others.

THE SIX LENSES OF ENGAGEMENT

WHAT THE CEO DID

After the front-line employee's unenthusiastic reception of the communication team members' PowerPoint presentations, the CEO had his team members conduct a series of focus groups with these employees over lunches. The goal was to identify why they might even care about the idea of The New Acme and, especially, why they might want to act on that idea. For the sake of simplicity, the CEO discussed the findings of his communication team from the perspectives of the same three representative employees used in the previous steps. The following example identifies the one or two lenses most important to each of these employees, and what they found meaningful in the idea of The New Acme.

WIFM* FROM THE PERSPECTIVES OF REPRESENTATIVE EMPLOYEES OR OTHER STAKEHOLDERS *"WHAT'S IN IT FOR ME?"	PROFESSIONAL VALUES	TEAM	ORGANIZATION	PERSONAL VALUES	FAMILY	SOCIETY
THE EMPLOYEE WHO ARRANGES EXPRESS DELIVERIES		X	X	X		

WIFM: The opportunity to contribute to a team and organization that wants to "do the right thing," and being appreciated by team members.

THE INSIDE SALES REP					X	

WIFM: Having clear goals and expectations tied to financial rewards and career progression.

THE FRONT LINE SUPERVISOR IN THE PLANT		X	X			

WIFM: This is her first position of leadership and she is excited about building a strong team in support of a CEO she respects.

WHAT THE CEO WAS THINKING

The discussion of these three representative employees sparked thoughtful discussions of what motivated employees to do a good job at Acme, and they were quickly able to apply these observations to other groups and situations. Here are the insights they gained from discussing each of these:

The Team and Organization Lenses were important to both the express shipping employee and the new supervisor. Discussions with these representative employees, and others like them, showed the new CEO that he had already been making an impact with his obvious concern for developing a quality organization by relying on and supporting his employees. However, the CEO also recognized that this enthusiasm could quickly fade without additional follow-up, and that the idea of The New Acme could provide a vehicle for turning this enthusiasm into meaningful action.

The Personal Values Lens was important to the shipping employee because he simply liked to do a good job. He actually had been getting frustrated because he had little clarity about what success looked like for his position and he received little feedback on the quality of his work. He saw the idea of The New Acme as a means of providing this clarity and the possibility for being recognized for his contributions.

The Family Lens was the most important for the inside sales rep. He had a single-minded focus on building the nest egg he needed to raise his young family and to build a house. He was quoted as saying, in the focus group, "Frankly, I could care less about what the rest of the organization does—Just give me a quota and point me in the right direction, and I'll bring in the sales." The CEO realized that there would be many people like this in the organization who would not appreciate the idea of The New Acme, but would appreciate the clarity of expectations it would bring with it.

WHAT ARE YOU THINKING?

If you have already collected data that will help you with the following exercise, pick out just a few representative employees on which to focus your attention—you can always expand the list later. If you are doing this from the perspective of your desk or armchair, it will still be useful to imagine two or three specific employees and try to see the idea of The-Organization-You-Lead through the lenses you think they would most likely use.

EXERCISE

REPRESENTATIVE EMPLOYEES OR OTHER STAKEHOLDERS	PROFESSIONAL VALUES	TEAM	ORGANIZATION	PERSONAL VALUES	FAMILY	SOCIETY
PERSON #1:						
WIFM:						
PERSON #2:						
WIFM:						
PERSON #3:						
WIFM:						

SUMMARY OF ENGAGING THE IDEA OF THE-ORGANIZATION-YOU-LEAD

Imagine a finely-designed, well-tuned race car, fully fuelled, its engine revved up. It has the potential to speed forward and perhaps win the race. But, it won't get anywhere if the transmission does not engage the engine with the wheels. The same is true for the idea of The-Organization-You-Lead. It may be a powerful idea, but if you haven't found the means of engaging the idea with the hearts and minds as well as the hands and feet of your employees, it's not going to go anywhere.

Your role as a leader is to understand how and why your employees choose to become engaged with the idea of The-Organization-You-Lead and to craft that idea, and your delivery of it, so that its power is transferred into business results through the behavior of your people. You achieve this not only by understanding the lenses through which they view your idea, but also by crafting the Focus, Shape and Alignment of your idea to maximize the efficiency with which the idea of your organization can be engaged.

Your Next Step:
Create An Action Plan

The default approach to defining the idea of The-Organization-You-Lead is to accept without much questioning the accumulated assumptions, preconceptions and myths by which people know it. In fact, as discussed in the introductory chapter, these generally accepted Foundational Beliefs and Values provide the organization with strength and stability. However, because these foundational ideas have acquired so much momentum, they will inexorably drag you into an idea of the future that, perhaps, was reasonable in years past but is no longer relevant to the future that is upon you. This is why it is essential that you and your team members regularly pause to re-examine the idea of The-Organization-You-Lead, to question its Focus, its Shape, its Alignment and its Engagement with those on whom you depend to move the organization forward. The CEO of Acme chose a very opportune moment to do this—the merging of three existing organizations, each with its own foundational beliefs and values, into a single new organization with a unified Future Vision and a common view of itself and of its leadership. Of course, journeys like this are never smooth and there will always be conflicts and tensions among ideas. But, using the Idea Leadership framework gave him a method for systematically addressing these issues with his team as they developed the idea of the organization, its Future Vision and the other ideas that defined it and carried it forward.

The exercises in this chapter are designed to support you in similar efforts. As you contemplate your next steps, consider discussing each of the exercises with your team members and asking the hard questions they represent. As you emerge from those exercises, you will find that you will have confirmed the majority of the Foundational Ideas you already hold about your organization. At the same time, you will almost certainly identify areas of disagreement you didn't realize you had as well as areas of ambiguity that need to be clarified. You can now see why the time you take to do this will undoubtedly pay off in the increased efficiency with which the organization achieves its purpose because of a tighter Focus, a more effective Shape, more efficient Alignment and, especially, a higher level of Engagement with the members of your team and their employees.

NOW WHAT?

Now that you have given careful thought to the idea of The-Organization-You-Lead, look over your analysis and identify some specific things you can do to increase the effectiveness of that idea. You may want to skim through some of the previous chapters for helpful hints, particularly in terms of the detailed success and risk factors.

EXERCISE

TASK	COMPLETION DATE

CHAPTER 6
The Idea of You-As-Leader

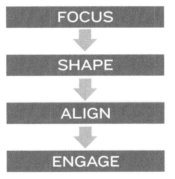

FOCUS

SHAPE

ALIGN

ENGAGE

THE IDEA OF
YOU-AS-LEADER
IN A NUTSHELL

Your role as a leader is to understand who you are as a leader and to communicate that idea with the people you lead.

KEY POINTS

- If you haven't carefully thought recently about who you are as a leader, these thoughts are probably a bit cloudy and unfocused, which will lead to unfocused thought and action among your employees and other stakeholders. This chapter will help you refine who you think you are, and people will know what you think through your actions.

- The idea of You-as-Leader is subject to the same principles as ideas delivered by organizational initiatives and other processes:

    Focus: You will be more effective if you first think through the purpose you want the idea of You-as-Leader to serve, and what actions you want specific people to take in response to it.

    Shape: When you are aware of the shape of the idea others hold of You-as-Leader, you can manage it to fit the circumstances.

    Alignment: The idea of You-as-Leader automatically provides a lot of momentum to any idea associated with it. Alignment between it and other key ideas will increase the net impact on your organization.

    Engagement: Your power comes from your people. Their engagement with the idea of You-as-Leader will determine the efficiency with which this power can move your organization forward.

Case Study: Observe how Joan Smith, the new Chief Security Officer at BigRetail, Inc. defines herself as leader and carves out a position of power during her first 90 days with the company.

Exercise: You may assess and develop the idea of You-as-Leader as you follow Ms. Smith on her trek toward a meaningful role at BigRetail, Inc.

HOW DO OTHERS THINK ABOUT YOU?

How do people in your organization think about you? What image comes to their minds when they see your name on an email? When they see you in the halls? In your executive team meetings? In the board room? What image comes to your mind when you think of you?

Most people don't know the answer to these questions. Most people aren't even sure how they think of themselves. Few people think about it and, if they do, they don't know what to do with that information.

If you have been in the same position in the same organization for a number of years, doing roughly the same things, the one thing you know for sure is that people have formed a fairly consistent image of who you are and what you stand for. If you are new to the organization or your position, or if you are trying some new approaches to your leadership, or if you are interacting with new people, the idea others hold of you is in flux. It is always possible to change the way people think about you, but you have the greatest opportunity for doing so when their ideas are in this malleable state.

The same is true for the idea that you hold of You-as-Leader. If you are like most people, this view of yourself is at least several years out of date, perhaps more than a decade (and this chapter will help you assess whether this is the case). This is because this idea is based on many years of experience with yourself as a leader and you have acquired some habits of thought—some of which may have worked for you in the past but probably aren't as useful in the present. Whatever idea you have of yourself is the idea you portray to others, and this has an impact on how they think of you and respond to you.

This chapter will help you redirect the tools you have learned so you can step back and think about how you view yourself and how others view you—just as you did with respect to the idea of The-Organization-You-Lead in the previous chapter. More important, you are now in a position where you can do something about the idea of You-as-Leader, following the same Four-Step Method you have used before.

STEP 1: FOCUS THE IDEA OF YOU-AS-LEADER

When you present the idea of You-as-Leader, you will be more effective if you first think through the purpose you want that idea to serve, and what actions you want specific people to take in response to it. This is particularly important when you have limited face-time with people who must decide quickly how they are going to respond.

STEP 2: SHAPE THE IDEA OF YOU-AS-LEADER

The level of precision and complexity of the idea people hold about you will be different in a times of crisis versus times that require strategic thinking. When you are aware of the shape of the idea others hold of You-as-Leader, you can manage it to fit the circumstances.

STEP 3: ALIGN THE IDEA OF YOU-AS-LEADER

By virtue of your power as a leader, any idea associated with you automatically has a lot of momentum. How you align the idea of You-as-Leader with other ideas in the organization, including other ideas you have previously delivered, has a large impact on the net momentum of your organization.

STEP 4: ENGAGE THE IDEA OF YOU-AS-LEADER

The only power you have as a leader comes to you through your people. The degree to which they have become engaged with the idea of You-as-Leader is directly related to the efficiency with which this power can move your organization forward.

As in the previous chapter on the idea of The-Organization-You-Lead, this chapter will walk you through the Four-Step Method. As you assess the idea of You-as-Leader, you will also see the steps that Ms. Joan Smith, Ph.D., took in her new role as chief security officer of BigRetail, Inc. You'll see her take up the challenge of thinking out and delivering an idea of Herself-as-Leader during the first 90 days of her tenure in a new organization—90 days being what many people consider to be the length of a new executive's honeymoon period as she settles into her new position.

Prior To Step 1:
Put Your Stake In The Ground

Have you ever been asked, "So, tell me a little about yourself?" This is often a first break-the-ice question in an interview for a job or new position and an applicant who is not ready for it is likely to talk too long and about the wrong things. If there was ever a time to think carefully of the idea of yourself, this would be it. But, this question is implicitly asked in almost any first meeting, whether business or social, and the appropriate answer to that question is dependent on the context in which it is asked. This is why it is useful to put some initial boundaries around the idea of You-as-Leader before you interact with those who do want to know, "Who are you and what do you stand for?"

Of course, the name of the idea of yourself is your own name. But, this is a good time to add a descriptor to begin to focus how you want others to think of you, as a leader, in this context. Is it "John Black, CEO?" or "John Black, Strategic Thinker," or "John Black, the guy who cares about his people?" or "John Black, the scratch golfer?" You can obviously think of scores of possibilities, but the people with whom you interact will only be able to remember a couple—and, if they mention you to someone else, they are likely to use only one.

WHAT MS. SMITH DID

Joan Smith, Ph.D., had to think through this issue when she took over as Chief Security Officer of BigRetail. She felt she had to take maximum advantage of a new executive's typical 90-day honeymoon period to establish the idea of Herself-as-Leader among the executive team and her direct reports. The example provides more detail on this situation and how Ms. Smith approached it.

JOAN SMITH, CHIEF SECURITY OFFICER: BACKGROUND

Joan Smith's position of Chief Security Officer at BigRetail, Inc. had been newly created by the CEO (who also headed the search process) in response to a serious security event—a hacker attack, and the loss of customer data due to an insider's subterfuge. These events at BigRetail had never been made public, but a number of similar events at competitors had made the headlines.

Prior to joining BigRetail, Ms. Smith had never held an executive position in a large retail organization. She had spent the previous 25 years of her career in various academic positions in several prestigious universities and government agencies, during which time she led a number of significant multi-year, multi-million dollar grants in the area of retail security. She was frequently called upon to assist in security crises for major corporations and regularly served on high-level advisory boards for both government and industry.

Landing this job was a career coup for Ms. Smith. The CEO selected her from a tough field of contenders, including the current CIO. Ms. Smith got the job on the basis of the very strong recommendations of several CEO's and CIO's who had participated on these advisory boards or for whom Ms. Smith had provided significant consulting services. Nevertheless, Ms. Smith recognized that her lack of corporate executive experience posed some significant challenges to her credibility within the organization.

Ms. Smith completed the name & process section of this exercise as follows:

WHAT DO YOU NAME THIS IDEA? Chief Security Officer, Ms. Joan Smith

WHAT ARE THE PROCESSES BY WHICH YOU WILL DELIVER THIS IDEA TO THE ORGANIZATION?
A ninety-day plan; a 90-day report to the CEO; interactions with the rest of the Executive Team—particularly the CIO and CFO, and Interactions with my staff.

WHAT MS. SMITH WAS THINKING

How Joan Smith named the idea of Herself-as-Leader: Notice that Joan left her Ph.D. title out of the idea of herself. Although she was very proud of this achievement and it had gained her a lot of credibility as an external expert, she felt it would emphasize her academic background at the expense of her credibility as an executive. Furthermore, each of the executive team members held an MBA, except for the CIO who had accumulated his extensive practical knowledge through the school of hard knocks, and she wanted to avoid being viewed as someone one who might value formal credentials over experience. This doesn't mean she wanted to hide the fact that she had this advanced degree, but that she wanted people to think first about her other characteristics when they heard her name.

When Joan first completed this form, she rather naturally wrote "Ms. Joan Smith, Chief Security Officer." But, as she thought about it, she realized that it was more important to her that people understand her role as Chief Security Officer—a position new to the organization—than they understand anything else about her. This is why she reversed the order on the form.

These may seem like insignificant details, but they aren't. They helped Joan decide how she wanted people to think about her, talk about her and interact with her: Not Joan Smith, the ex-academic; not Joan Smith, the interesting new person on the executive team; but rather, The New Chief Security Officer, whose name is Joan Smith. Of course, this also helped her to understand how she wanted to think about her new self.

How Joan Smith planned to deliver the idea of Herself-as-Leader: Joan recognized that she would be delivering the idea of herself every minute of every hour she was on the job. However, this exercise helped her to focus on some key situations so she could think about this challenge carefully. She knew that if she could effectively deliver the idea of herself in these limited situations, she would more effectively deliver it in most other situations. She also knew that, if she were unsuccessful in delivering the idea of Herself-as-Leader in these situations, she wouldn't be able to succeed in her new position.

WHAT ARE YOU THINKING?

Now, identify the name to which you will refer to the idea of You-as-Leader, for the purpose of this exercise, and the principal ways you will deliver this idea to the organization. Note that you may wish to fine-tune your responses to these two questions as you complete the remainder of this exercise.

EXERCISE

What do you name this idea (The Idea of You-as-Leader)?

What are the processes by which you will deliver this idea to the organization? (Limit to a maximum of 3)

Step 1:
Focus The Idea Of You-As-Leader

This step will help you identify the Purpose, Actors and Actions associated with the idea of You-as-Leader. It will probably feel strange, to think of the idea of You-as-Leader as having a purpose that results in specific people taking specific actions. But, this is what happens whether you think about it or not. Thinking about the focus of the idea of You-as-Leader will make you more conscious of this reality so you can make deliberate choices to adjust that focus when necessary. For clarity, I have broken down this step into two parts.

Step 1-A:
Identify the Purpose Of The Idea of You-as-Leader

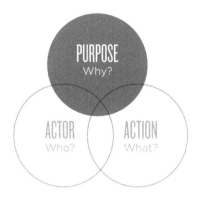

The purpose of the idea of You-as-Leader is the same as the purpose of your leadership. What do you want to accomplish as a leader, in general and in specific circumstances? Why is this important to your organization strategically and tactically? Why is it important to you in terms of your role in the organization, your career and your life? Questions of purpose are very tough questions. Most people don't think about them, operating on autopilot until one day they stop and ask themselves, "Wait a minute! What am I doing here? Why is it worth it?"

When I take on a coaching engagement, even if the executive wants to work on a very specific problem such as communications or team relationships, it doesn't take more than a couple of weeks for the individual to come face-to-face with the question, "So, what do I want to accomplish in this role?" A little later in the process another question can come up: "What am I trying to accomplish with my life?" Without answers to these basic questions, it is possible to address only short-term concerns, often avoiding the root issues. While this sort of tactical approach to dealing with the idea of You-as-Leader will keep you focused on your quarterly and annual objectives, it can also prevent you from standing back and looking at the big picture. When this happens, you allow the idea of You-as-Leader to be formed by your circumstances rather than your thoughtful choices.

WHAT MS. SMITH DID

The following case example describes how Ms. Smith defined the purpose of the idea of Herself-as-Leader.

THE PURPOSE OF THE IDEA OF
CHIEF SECURITY OFFICER, MS. JOAN SMITH

IMMEDIATE OBJECTIVE:

I will be perceived as a competent executive with the power base I need to build an integrated security strategy; the CEO, the CFO and the CIO will each perceive me as a strong team member; I will have the trust of my direct reports

LONG-TERM PURPOSE:

Keep BigRetail out of the news by creating and implementing an integrated approach to security that crosses all corporate functions including, but not limited to, information services. I also want to lay the foundation for a new career direction in which I can more actively practice what I have been preaching for over 25 years.

WHAT THE MS. SMITH WAS THINKING

Ms. Smith's long-term purpose was clear. She had based her entire academic and consulting career on the philosophy that the only way to have effective security within a large organization is to integrate the efforts of all segments of the organization, both technical and non-technical. She now wanted to demonstrate the method for accomplishing this, for the sake of the organization and for the sake or her own evolving career. However, she knew that the only way she could achieve that long-term, cross-organizational objective was to first develop a strong political powerbase, the foundation of which was the trust and support of the CEO, the CFO and the CIO.

WHAT ARE YOU THINKING?

Now, identify the short-term impact and the long-term purpose of the idea you are going to deliver, i.e., the idea of You-as-Leader. Remember, keeping it simple will help you to identify your highest priorities.

EXERCISE

What is the long-term purpose of the idea you named at the beginning of this exercise? (Limit to one):

What are the short-term objectives of this idea? (Maximum of three):

Step 1-B:
Define Who You Want to Take What Actions in Response to the Idea of You-as-Leader

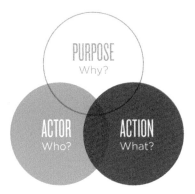

Identifying the actions you expect from a limited set of representative individuals forces you to be quite clear about what you are trying to accomplish as you deliver to the organization the idea of You-as-Leader.

At this point, it is important to distinguish between the concept of influence and that of manipulation. As a leader, you are constantly influencing the thought and actions of others. It is your job to do so. Given this responsibility, it is better to do this consciously rather than to simply allow it to happen—which is the point of this exercise. Manipulation does attempt to affect the behavior of people, but can aim toward a selfish purpose achieved at the expense of others. Influence is also distinguished from manipulation in how it relates to trust and transparency. The clearer you can be with people about what you would like them to do, and why, the more likely they will be willing to act as you wish. This is because people pretty quickly sniff out hidden purposes and, once the idea of You-as-Leader becomes associated with manipulation, your power to influence will be severely limited. Clarifying for yourself the actions you want people to take, and why, is the function of this exercise.

WHAT MS. SMITH DID

The following example describes how Ms. Smith approached the task of identifying the representative Actors and Actions intended in response to the Idea of Chief Security Officer, Ms. Joan Smith.

REPRESENTATIVE ACTOR	ACTION
THE CEO	He will approve my Year 1 plan and budget; He will demonstrate to the Executive Team that I have his trust.
THE CIO	He will share information with me and partner with me to execute my security strategy.
THE CFO	He will ask me questions during executive meetings and listen to my answers.
MY DIRECT REPORTS	They will watch my back and actively support and execute my security strategy.

WHAT MS. SMITH WAS THINKING

Ms. Smith felt she already had the trust of the CEO. But she also knew she needed to cement that trust with his buy-in to a clear plan and budget.

On the other hand, she realized from the start that the CIO was not on her side and that she would have to work hard to gain his support. She felt that the best evidence of this support would be if he would willingly share information and coordinate plans with her, which is why Joan made it a target behavior.

Joan felt that the CFO was recognized by the other executives as the second-most powerful person in the room and that his approval would be a significant political force on her behalf. But, he played his cards close to his chest, listening much more than talking, very carefully expressing explicit support for the positions of others. For this reason, Joan felt it would be a significant victory if he would publicly demonstrate his respect for her opinions through their interactions in executive team meetings—which would also have a positive ripple effect as word of his stamp of approval would spread.

Joan was able to select most of her direct reports, because hers was a new role. She made sure all of them were knowledgeable about the organization and were well connected. They would act as her eyes and ears. She knew that their insights and support were critical for her to gain and maintain a foothold in an organization about which she knew little.

For the first 90 days, Jane regularly glanced at this list of actors and actions as a means of measuring her progress towards achieving the purpose of the idea of Herself-as-Leader.

WHAT ARE YOU THINKING?

Now, complete the same activity for the idea of You-as-Leader. Remember that your goal is to identify a limited number of specific, representative actors and actions that best demonstrate how the purpose of your idea can be achieved. The more specific you can be, the easier it will be for you to track your own progress.

EXERCISE

Actors and Actions: Identify three representative employees or stakeholders and indicate one specific action you will want each to take upon accepting your idea of You-as-Leader and integrating it into their work.

REPRESENTATIVE ACTOR	ACTION
PERSON #1:	
PERSON #2:	
PERSON #3:	

SUMMARY OF FOCUSING THE IDEA OF YOU-AS-LEADER

Most leaders don't take the time to methodically think about who they are and what they want to achieve—in their careers or in their lives in general. Yet, from the perspective of what you have read in the previous chapters, you can see the very tight connection between how a leader views herself and how those she leads respond to her. There is an equally tight connection between how people view the leader and how they view her organization.

As a leader, you must fully understand the business impact you want the idea of You-as-Leader to have on your constituents and you must frequently check in and ask yourself if you are achieving that impact. If the impact is less than you would like, you can use the remaining steps in this exercise, and the information you read about Focus in Chapter 1, to help you to determine what you can do about it.

Step 2:
Shape The Idea Of You-As-Leader

Make a list of five or six leaders you know well, perhaps those executives with whom you work most closely. Now, see where the idea you hold of each of them as a leader falls into each of the categories of shape in the diagram below. As you do this, you will find that your assessment will depend on the situation in which you envision them, but you will also see how you can differentiate them from each other in terms of the tendency of each to lean towards one or the other boxes.

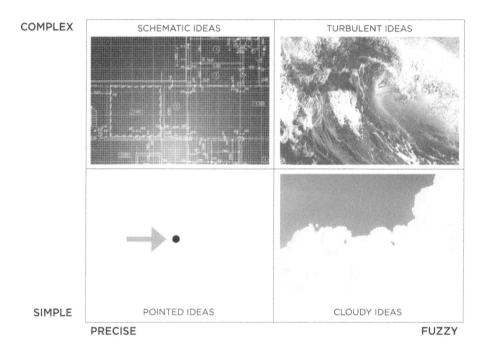

COMPLEX

SCHEMATIC IDEAS

TURBULENT IDEAS

SIMPLE

POINTED IDEAS

CLOUDY IDEAS

PRECISE

FUZZY

Now, imagine into which box each of these people would put you and ask yourself, "Is this shape of the idea of myself as leader the most useful shape?" and "Is it consistent with the shape of my own idea of myself as leader?" and, especially, "Are there situations in which I would be more effective if I nudged the shape of that idea in one direction or another?" Information about how others view you is often difficult to obtain, which is why people sometimes ask a coach or other third party to collect it through interviews, observations and/or surveys.

The following step is intended to help you think through these questions. Again, you will be able to follow the path Ms. Smith took as she thought about the shape of the idea of Herself-as-Leader, as held in the minds of those she most wanted to influence. Remember, the Shape of the idea of Ms. Smith-as-Leader will determine the ease with which people can pick it up, carry it around and hand it off to others.

WHAT MS. SMITH DID

In order to fine tune her approach to delivering the idea of Herself-as-Leader, Ms. Smith considered the shape of that idea from the perspective of each of several constituents and thought about how that shape might be adjusted for the idea to achieve its purpose. The following chart summarizes her observations:

EMPLOYEE OR OTHER STAKEHOLDER	SHAPE OF IDEA AS CURRENTLY PERCEIVED (Circle one)	HOW SHAPE SHOULD BE MODIFIED FOR THIS INDIVIDUAL (Circle one in each column)	
THE CEO	(Pointed) Cloudy Turbulent Schematic	More Precise (Keep as-is) More Fuzzy	More Simple Keep as-is (More Complex)
THE CIO	Pointed Cloudy (Turbulent) Schematic	(More Precise) Keep as-is More Fuzzy	(More Simple) Keep as-is More Complex
THE CFO	Pointed Cloudy Turbulent (Schematic)	More Precise (Keep as-is) More Fuzzy	(More Simple) Keep as-is More Complex
MY DIRECT REPORTS	Pointed (Cloudy) Turbulent Schematic	(More Precise) Keep as-is More Fuzzy	More Simple Keep as-is (More Complex)

WHAT MS. SMITH WAS THINKING

Ms. Smith recognized from the start, even during her job interviews, that the CEO had a rather narrow perspective on her role, repeatedly using the phrase several board members had used with him: "Keep us out of the news!" She regarded this perspective of her role as rather pointed and, in particular, overly simplistic. While understanding the importance of this goal, she saw appearing in the news as a symptom of a set of problems that could only be avoided with a deeper understanding of the complexity of the issue—and of her role as a leader. She resolved to accomplish this by gradually helping him to understand the variety of root causes of security breaches and of both technical and non-technical solutions for them.

From the CIO's perspective, the idea of Ms. Smith was a turbulent one. Ms. Smith recognized during her interviews that the CIO was unsure what an academic would bring to the table that he himself couldn't provide. She found him to be defensive and, in fact, the CEO had warned her that the CIO had taken his decision to hire Ms. Smith rather personally. Ms. Smith recognized that she would have to take the turbulence out of his perception of Herself-as-Leader. She decided to do this by presenting a simple and precise description of how she viewed the relationship between her role and his role. In particular, she wanted him to understand exactly how she thought she could help him achieve his own objectives—and how she needed to rely on his expertise to accomplish hers. She knew this would take time, but she also knew it was necessary for establishing the trusting collaborative relationship she needed to be successful.

The CFO was extremely detail-oriented in everything he did. During Ms. Smith's interview, he had grilled her for two hours on her resume—asking details of specific projects, of her various skill sets and, particularly her understanding of the fine points of particular financial issues. When the interview was finished, she felt he was familiar with every detail on her 8-page academic resume, but that he did not yet understand exactly how she would apply those skills to BigRetail's security issues. She decided that she needed to trim the detail out of his precise, complex view of Herself-as-Leader. She wanted him to have an equally precise but simpler view of her intended approach to security and how it related to financial issues. She planned to do this with a relatively simple graphic model of the relationships between the specific security issues she was going to address and financial outcomes. She would back this up with a spreadsheet with data he could manipulate to examine her logic more carefully.

Ms. Smith's direct reports had only a relatively cloudy idea of her as leader. They had met her as a group over wine and cheese, and she seemed like a friendly and people-oriented person, but they knew little else about her. Ms. Smith recognized that this initial simple, fuzzy perspective of her was fine as a start. But, she also knew she wanted them to have a much clearer understanding of how she intended to approach her role as leader. In particular, she wanted them to know, in some level of detail, her expectations for each of them. She soon had one-on-one discussions with them to understand what they had to offer, what roles they would prefer to play, and how they could best support each other. She documented these discussions in detailed job descriptions and performance expectations to cover the first three months, until they got to know each other better.

WHAT ARE YOU THINKING?

Now, take a close look at the idea of You-as-Leader you described in Steps 1-3, from the perspective of one or more people who you need to accept delivery of your idea, and decide if there is anything you should do to adjust its shape.

Assess the shape of the Idea of You-as-Leader from the perspective of others:

a. Identify one or more representative employees or other stakeholders who you hope will take action on your idea.

b. For each person:
    - Indicate the shape of your idea as that individual currently sees it.
    - Indicate, for that person, if the idea needs to be reshaped on the simple-complex or precise-ambiguous dimensions.

EMPLOYEE OR OTHER STAKEHOLDER	SHAPE OF IDEA AS CURRENTLY PERCEIVED (Circle one)	HOW SHAPE SHOULD BE MODIFIED FOR THIS INDIVIDUAL (Circle one in each column)	
PERSON #1:	Pointed Cloudy Turbulent Schematic	More Precise Keep as-is More Fuzzy	More Simple Keep as-is More Complex
PERSON #2:	Pointed Cloudy Turbulent Schematic	More Precise Keep as-is More Fuzzy	More Simple Keep as-is More Complex
PERSON #3:	Pointed Cloudy Turbulent Schematic	More Precise Keep as-is More Fuzzy	More Simple Keep as-is More Complex

SUMMARY OF SHAPING THE IDEA OF YOU-AS-LEADER

The shape of the idea people have of you has a large impact on how they interact with you and how they talk to others about you. For example, a cloudy perspective is just fine for the "getting to know you" stage of a relationship but is not very useful when it is time to get down to serious business discussions. At the same time, it is in these kinds of initial interactions when a carefully crafted, simple and precise 30-second elevator speech can set up expectations for future business relationships.

Your role as a leader is to recognize the shape of the idea people have of you, and its implications for your success, and to make the necessary adjustments—often on the spur of the moment. These impressions are particularly important if you are a busy executive because the time available to deliver the idea of You-as-Leader, especially one-to-one, is often very limited.

Step 3: Align The Idea Of You-As-Leader

The more momentum the idea of You-as-Leader accumulates, the more you will have the power to influence people and events, the power to drive through turbulence, the power to excite, and the power to move the organization forward. You will always bring some momentum with you when you first arrive at an organization. This will be based on the strength of your reputation, the endorsement of others and even the power of your personality. But, that momentum will dissipate quickly unless you find ways to align the idea of You-as-Leader with existing high-momentum ideas within the organization. This is why it is important to search out these high-momentum ideas and determine with which you want to be closely associated in the minds of your employees, and from which you will want distance yourself. As always, the first thing you need to do is to scan the organization for aligned and non-aligned ideas that may help or hinder the idea of You-as-Leader. Watch how Ms. Smith approached this task in the crucial first 90 days on the job as the new Chief Security Officer.

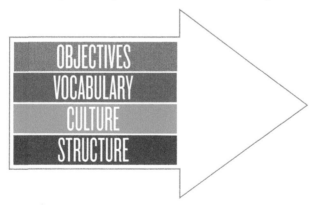

WHAT MS. SMITH DID

As in most organizations, the culture was already structured around a number of key ideas accumulated over previous years. For her purposes, Ms. Smith identified four security-related ideas that permeated not just the executive team, but the organization as a whole. She realized she needed to take these ideas into account as she crafted the idea of Herself-as-Leader of the new security function. She rated each in terms of their alignment, or misalignment, with how she wanted people to think of her in her new leadership position. In the following example, "A" indicates alignment and "M" indicates misalignment.

OTHER IDEAS IN THE ORGANIZATION THAT MAY BE RELEVANT TO THE IDEA OF YOU-AS-LEADER	OBJECTIVES	VOCABULARY	CULTURE	STRUCTURE
RISK MANAGEMENT	A	A	A	A
INFORMATION SECURITY	M	M	M	
ORGANIZATIONAL STABILITY	A			
SECURITY AS A COST			M	

WHAT MS. SMITH WAS THINKING

The idea of Risk Management had been introduced to the organization several years ago, Ms. Smith discovered, through a very successful initiative intended to encourage all employees to take responsibility for managing risk in three key areas: inventory shrinkage (theft), customer and employee safety, and loss of customers to e-commerce. When Ms. Smith arrived, risk management in these three areas was routinely included in performance metrics and the idea had been thoroughly accepted by the organization. Ms. Smith saw a strong connection between this approach to risk management and her approach to security risk management. The two approaches were tightly aligned in terms of their financial objectives, the vocabulary of risk management, a culture that recognized that risk management was everyone's responsibility and a structure that integrated the idea into performance management systems. She realized that aligning the idea of herself with the idea of Risk Management would help people understand her philosophy from a perspective with which they were already familiar.

The idea of Information Security, as currently understood within the organization, posed a bit of a barrier to how Ms. Smith wanted people to think of her. People at BigRetail—and especially the CIO—tended to think that the primary objective of information security was to respond to external threats, primarily those of hackers. However, when Ms. Smith used that term—a term she normally associated with her role—she referred to a much broader set of threats, both internal and external. She realized that she would either have to make a concerted effort to change the meaning of that term within the organization, or find a word or phrase other than "information security" that would better describe what she stood for. She decided that the latter option made more sense.

The idea of Organizational Stability was an underlying concern of all employees—from the executive suite to the stockroom—who had been witnessing store closings and layoffs at competitive companies. Ms. Smith recognized organizational stability as an important concern of her security function and realized that making a conscious effort to align that idea with the idea of Herself-as-Leader would help everyone to view her in a positive light.

The idea of Security as a Cost was reflected in budget negotiations from the store level through districts and regions. When something needed to be cut, the short-term expediency of cutting back on security expenses was often turned to first. Ms. Smith preferred to think of security as an investment with real paybacks. She realized that the idea of Security as a Cost was deeply embedded in the culture and would have to be taken into account as she developed policies and procedures that had implications for the budgets of individual profit centers. She also realized that to bring about the changes she envisioned she needed the idea of Herself-as-Leader to be aligned with the idea of organizational investment and profit.

WHAT ARE YOU THINKING?

Now, go through the same process with the idea of You-as-Leader, as you have defined it in previous exercises.

EXERCISE

Assess the degree of alignment of other ideas in the organization with the idea of You-as-Leader:

  a. List other ideas in the organization that may be relevant to the idea of You-as-Leader.

  b. Identify the degree to which each is aligned to the idea of You-as-Leader on each of the four facets of alignment, using the following code:
    • A = The idea is aligned with yours (works with your idea)
    • M = The idea is misaligned with yours (works against your idea)
    • Blank = neutral or uncertain

OTHER IDEAS IN THE ORGANIZATION THAT MAY BE RELEVANT TO THE IDEA OF YOU-AS-LEADER	OBJECTIVES	VOCABULARY	CULTURE	STRUCTURE

SUMMARY OF ALIGNING THE IDEA OF YOU-AS-LEADER

The idea of You-as-Leader is only one idea in a sea of ideas within your organization. Some of these are drifting, or being driven, in the direction you wish to go while others are not. From this perspective, you can see how important it is to identify ideas moving in the direction you desire, as the people who are attached to them will quickly become your allies. By the same token, you can see the importance of identifying those ideas moving in opposite directions. If you neglect to remain vigilant in this way, you will most likely miss opportunities to take advantage of the momentum driving other ideas, or you may be inadvertently pulled in the wrong direction.

Your role as a leader is to remain aware of the currents of ideas within your organization, particularly those under the surface, so you know which you should steer into and which you should avoid. Your goal is to have the idea of You-as-Leader to continually gain momentum with as little expenditure of your limited resources as possible.

Step 4:
Engage Others With The Idea
Of You-As-Leader

The idea of You-as-Leader is clearly a very personal one, and thoughtful consideration of this idea will help you gain insight about who you are as a leader and as a person. Likewise, your employees are asking themselves the question, "What do I see as I view the idea of You-as-Leader through the personal lenses that define who I am?" How they answer will determine whether or not they are going to commit that extra 20% of themselves to the idea of You-as-Leader. The first thing to do, as you begin this step, is to view the idea of You-as-Leader through the lenses of others.

THE SIX LENSES OF ENGAGEMENT

WHAT MS. SMITH DID

Now observe how Ms. Smith managed to remain true to herself while also helping individuals see her through their own somewhat different lenses—and to recognize that a relationship would be mutually beneficial.

By working through the previous four steps of this exercise Ms. Smith was able to think about what was most important to each of the constituents who could provide support necessary for her success. Now she was ready to refine her thinking by looking at the idea of Herself-as-Leader from the lenses most favored by each and identify, from their perspective, "What's in it for me?". She summarized her thoughts in the following chart.

WIFM* FROM THE PERSPECTIVES OF REPRESENTATIVE EMPLOYEES OR OTHER STAKEHOLDERS *"WHAT'S IN IT FOR ME?"	PROFESSIONAL VALUES	TEAM	ORGANIZATION	PERSONAL VALUES	FAMILY	SOCIETY
THE CEO			X			
WIFM: The organization will be protected.						
THE CIO	X	X				
WIFM: The current information security philosophy will be supported and the stature of the information systems team will be enhanced.						
THE CFO	X		X			
WIFM: Financial health will increase, risk management will be more effective, and the organization will be more secure.						
MY DIRECT REPORTS		X		X		
WIFM: Team members will grow professionally, self-direction will be encouraged and there will be a collaborative team environment.						

WHAT MS. SMITH WAS THINKING

Ms. Smith listened carefully as she interacted with the people most important to her success in the first 90 days, and she also did background research. Here are the results of her thoughtful analysis of how each of these individuals would view the idea of Herself-as-Leader as they looked through the lenses most important to them. The question she knew that each would be asking, in its most elementary terms, was "What's in it for me?"

WIFM from the CEO's perspective. Ms. Smith decided that, by far, the lens the CEO considered most important was the organizational lens. He would support any idea that supported the strength and stability of his organization.

WIFM from the CIO's perspective. The CIO was less upset that he wasn't selected for the position than he was concerned that the CEO had questioned his professional credibility and that of his team. It was clear to Ms. Smith that the CIO had to see her as respectful and appreciative, as he viewed her through his professional and team lenses, if she was to turn him into an ally.

WIFM from the CFO's perspective. Ms. Smith recognized that the CFO was acutely aware of the expectations of the financial community and invested both personally and professionally in the financial success of the organization. She knew that if she could present the idea of Herself-as-Leader in these terms, she would have his support.

WIFM from her direct reports' perspectives. When building her team, Ms. Smith selected people because of the value they placed on teamwork and their commitment to personal growth and development. Knowing they would view the idea of Herself-as-Leader through the lenses of these values, and that they would detect that she held these same values, she expected that she would have their full commitment from the start.

WHAT ARE YOU THINKING?

You have probably already thought of many individuals in and outside of your organization whose ideas and actions matter to your success. For the following exercise, however, pick out just a few representative employees on which to focus your attention—you can always expand the list later. If you are doing this from the perspective of your desk or armchair, it will still be useful to imagine two or three specific employees and try to see the idea of You-as-Leader through the lenses you think they would most likely use.

EXERCISE

Determine the lens through which individuals are likely to view the idea of You-as-Leader to determine if they care about it:

  a. List several individuals who represent distinct employee or stakeholder groups who you need to engage with your idea of You-as-Leader.

  b. Identify with an 'X' the 1-2 lenses each person is likely to consider most important when evaluating your idea of You-as-Leader

  c. Indicate WIFM ("What's in it for me?") for each person to accept and act on your idea of You-as-Leader as you would like him to.

WIFM* FROM THE PERSPECTIVES OF REPRESENTATIVE EMPLOYEES OR OTHER STAKEHOLDERS *WHAT'S IN IT FOR ME?	PROFESSIONAL VALUES	TEAM	ORGANIZATION	PERSONAL VALUES	FAMILY	SOCIETY
PERSON #1:						
WIFM:						
PERSON #2:						
WIFM:						
PERSON #3:						
WIFM:						

SUMMARY OF ENGAGING THE IDEA OF YOU-AS-LEADER

Your idea of You-as-Leader is very tied up with your own ego—your own self image of who you are and who you want to be. This is a good thing, because it allows you to engage the momentum of your life and career to move the organization forward. At the same time, you are certainly aware of leaders who have allowed their egos to get in the way of their good judgment, particularly when the idea they hold of themselves clashes with the ideas others hold of them. This is something to avoid, because you don't want to be wasting your momentum by battling illusions.

Your role as leader is to understand the lenses through which you view yourself and others (and to occasionally clean and polish them) as well as the lenses others use to view you. You should strive to gain an objective perspective on your idea of You-as-Leader and of the ideas others hold of you—and of themselves.

Your Next Step:
Create An Action Plan

The idea of You-as-Leader is your most potent tool for achieving success for your organization, and for yourself. It will have momentum whether you do anything about it or not. That being the case, you need to ask the key questions: Is that momentum Focused in the direction you have chosen, or is it likely to be scattered in multiple directions? Does the idea of You-as-Leader have the shape that will allow people to pick it up, understand it, and do with it what you wish them to? Is the idea of You-as-Leader aligned with the ideas most important to you, particularly the idea of The-Organization-You-Lead and its Future Vision? And, most importantly, do you know what people see when they comprehend the idea of You-as-Leader from their individual perspectives and become engaged with it, or not? Without the engagement of the idea of You-as-Leader with the ideas most important to your employees, the Focus, Shape and Alignment of that idea is irrelevant.

However, the most important determinant of the potency of the idea of You-as-Leader is the degree to which you have a clear understanding of that idea yourself, of its Focus, Shape, Alignment and Engagement. Because if you don't have that level of clarity, your employees and other constituents cannot possibly have it either. Self understanding is the most important reason for you to go through the exercise of this chapter. Only then, can you go the next step to plan how to deliver the idea of You-as-Leader effectively to your organization.

NOW WHAT?

Now that you have given careful thought to the idea of You-as-Leader, look over your analysis and identify some specific things you can do to increase its effectiveness. You may want to skim through some of the previous chapters for helpful hints, particularly in terms of the detailed success and risk factors.

EXERCISE

TASK	COMPLETION DATE

CHAPTER 7
Balancing Tensions
Among Ideas

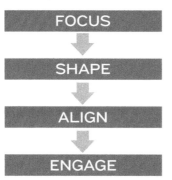

FOCUS

SHAPE

ALIGN

ENGAGE

BALANCING TENSIONS
IN A NUTSHELL

Your role as a leader is to grapple with the complicated, detailed, dynamic, and conflict-ridden reality that is organizational life and culture.

KEY POINTS

- Key ideas within an organization can never be totally aligned, and there may be significant tensions among them.

- It is far better to recognize and balance the tensions among the ideas that define you and your organization than to pretend that those tensions don't exist.

- The tensions among the values associated with an organization, and how those tensions are managed, define an organization's culture more than the values themselves.

Case Study: This brief chapter illustrates the above key points with the story of the demise of Arthur Andersen, the CPA partnership founded in 1913 that became one of the "Big Five" accounting firms before meeting an untimely end in August of 2002.

Contradictions are the Reality

The exercises in the previous two chapters required you to think about the idea of The-Organization-You-Lead and the idea of You-as-Leader in somewhat ideal terms: How you view yourself, how you would like others to view you, what you stand for and what you want to accomplish. In each of these exercises, you have undoubtedly discovered tensions between ideas of how you would like things to be and the practical reality you face on a day-to-day basis. For every value you claim for your organization, or for yourself, you will almost always claim another one that conflicts with it to some extent.

For example, consider the ideas of Analysis and Action—an organization may value both but, at the same time, will often find the one conflicting with the other. Likewise the ideas of Individual Initiative and Team Collaboration, or Quarterly Profit and Strategic Goals. This brings to mind the frequently stated though not totally accurate, expression, "We can give you high quality, low cost and speed—choose which two you want." These types of paradoxes are unavoidable as you create and foster the idea of The-Organization-You-Lead .

You face similar tensions when you craft the idea of You-as-Leader. For example, at a personal level, every leader must confront the idea of Work-Life Balance where the ideas of Dedication to the Organization and Dedication to Family are almost always in conflict to some degree. Likewise a leader frequently has to balance the natural tension between the equally valid ideas of Authoritative Control and Team Empowerment as he defines the idea of Himself-as-Leader.

Some leaders deal with these natural tensions by ignoring them or denying they exist. Others recognize that balancing the one off the other is an important part of their job as leader. Ignoring the tensions often feels like the easiest route because it avoids having to deal with difficult issues. However, leaders who choose this approach open themselves up to many of the risks you read about in Chapters 1-4. For example, ideas may become disconnected from reality if the facts of these tensions are ignored (Risk 1.2); or "feeling good" about an idea may become more important than dealing with its difficult realities (Risk 2.2); or ideas may collide silently because no one is paying attention to the fact that they are, in fact, in conflict with each other (Risk 3.3).

A virtue of using the processes outlined in this book is that the often natural and unavoidable tensions among equally valued ideas become apparent. As such, they will help you to approach leadership as the art of balancing ideas within your organization. The remainder of this chapter illustrates what is at stake for you and your organization when you embrace leadership as a balancing act—and what happens if you pretend it isn't. I'll return to the case of the Arthur Andersen organization, as its partners explored this balancing act during the eighties, and how they finally stumbled and fell in 2002.

ARTHUR ANDERSEN: A FALL FROM THE HIGH WIRE

Arthur Andersen was a CPA partnership founded in 1913 that became one of the "Big Five" accounting firms before meeting an untimely demise in August of 2002 as a result of the Enron debacle. In 1985, I assisted with a study of its organizational culture—this was several years after I conducted the audit of its training evaluation function I mentioned in Chapter 3. At the time, senior partners nearing retirement wanted to ensure that the younger generations of managers, consultants and partners recognized the traditional and strongly held values of the partnership—they believed that these values described the idea of the organization more than any set of procedures or practices. For them, there was a very strong overlap between ideas they held about themselves as leaders and the ideas they held about their organization. In fact, they believed it was the adherence to those commonly-held values that made the partnership a success. I helped analyze the interview data of several hundred members of Arthur Andersen from around the world, from administrative assistants to country managing partners, who were asked to identify its core values. The analysis resulted in a list of ten values:

- Client Service
- Hard Work
- The "One Firm" Concept
- Recruiting Quality People
- Training & Development

- Meritocracy
- Integrity
- Esprit de Corps
- Professional Leadership
- Stewardship: Investing in the Future

We duly reported these results to the board of senior partners. They accepted the results appreciatively, concluding that it was an accurate portrayal of their culture. For my part, although I agreed with the list of values, I disagreed that they defined the culture of the partnership. I took the stand that the culture is not defined as much by those ten values as it is by how the unavoidable tensions among those values are dealt with.

In the 1985 study, it was clear that the ideas of "Meritocracy" and "Esprit de Corps" were inherently in conflict with each other. The idea of Meritocracy included conducting fair and objective evaluations of their personnel and giving credit where credit was due. As you might expect, this led to intense competition among consultants and managers to make partner. In practice, this was reflected in an "up or out" philosophy where, if a young manager did not make partner in a certain number of years, he would be eased out. In this way, the idea of Meritocracy unavoidably conflicted with the equally sound and equally embraced idea of Esprit de Corps, which stressed the importance of helping out colleagues when in need, and putting the team ahead of self interests. Simultaneously managing both of these ideas was certainly a balancing act.

Because of the unavoidable reality of such conflicts, I argued that the culture of an organization is defined not by its core values, but by how the tensions among those values are managed. I told the executives at Arthur Andersen that, to be practical and credible, these ideas of who they were as leaders and what the organization stood for had to be recognized as requiring a balancing act. I gave them another example that held the seeds of potential conflict: The values of "Integrity" and "Client Service". In fact, this conflict eventually led to the organization's demise. The value of "Integrity" reflected the organization's role as a CPA firm and, as such, a protector of the public trust, and partners took this obligation extremely seriously. Arthur Andersen himself was said to have turned down major client engagements rather than risk being asked to cut corners on the client's behalf. At the same time, the value of "Client Service" unavoidably creates a tension with the value of "Integrity" within any CPA firm that is the guardian of the public trust. An example of this is when a partner makes a judgment in a gray area on the client's behalf that might conflict with the stance a truly objective auditor might otherwise take. This conflict became evident with disastrous results years later as the pressures of pleasing clients through the increasingly profitable revenue stream provided by consulting services began to push auditors to cut corners past the gray areas, resulting in a number of significant lawsuits. For Arthur Andersen, this conflict came to a head with the bankruptcy of the Enron Corporation. Many believe that the partnership's audit practices contributed to the ability of Enron to cover up its financial difficulties as long as it had. As Enron's auditor, Arthur Andersen was indicted and convicted of destroying evidence. Although this conviction was later overturned by the US Supreme Court, by then the damage had been done and the partnership was effectively dissolved. While the Enron scandal precipitated the final downfall of Arthur Andersen, it could be argued that the seeds of its failure were sown years earlier with the organization's failure to recognize and balance the unavoidable conflicts among its values.

THE MORAL OF THE STORY—RECOGNIZE AND MANAGE TENSIONS AMONG IDEAS

Whether you deliver an idea through an organizational initiative or a one-on-one conversation, no matter how well you manage its Focus, Shape, Alignment or Engagement, there will always be inconsistencies: different components of the same idea may conflict with each other and different people's perspectives on any idea you offer are likely to be at odds with each other. The multiple ideas you present to the organization will always conflict with each other to some degree.

Arthur Andersen confronted this reality with disastrous results. The moral of their story applies to you as an individual leader as well as to your organization as a whole. When you look at yourself or your organization through your own personal lenses, you will find that your values are intertwined with all of your ideas. For this reason, you will undoubtedly find natural conflicts among the ideas that define you, and that define your organization. The fact is, ideas never mesh as you would like them to. Reality is always messier than the ideas we formulate in our heads. Some individuals and organizations deal with such conflicts by ignoring them or pretending they don't exist, because it feels very uncomfortable to acknowledge these inconsistencies, particularly in a public forum.

Unfortunately, ignoring these natural conflicts leads to a general disregard for the ideas themselves, as well as the values they represent, and to perceptions of hypocrisy. What does it mean to your employees when you portray yourself as a supporter of work-life balance and then require them to come in on weekends? Or that you are loyal to your employees and then you lay off 20% of them? These actions will be seen as hypocritical unless you have made it clear that part of taking ideas seriously is wrestling with the tensions among them. This balancing act is part of your job, and part of the job of each of your employees.

LEADING THROUGH IDEAS ON THE HIGH WIRE

We started this book by recognizing that ideas live in a survival of the fittest environment, and that the role of the leader is to assess and mitigate the risks faced by strategic ideas. We focused on those ideas that are delivered to the organization through the processes of corporate initiatives, but also saw how the principles of idea leadership apply to ideas with short, as well as long, time horizons. We examined how ideas work in terms of a four-step method, and then we expanded the scope of that method by applying it to the idea of You-as-Leader and the idea of The-Organization-You-Lead.

As promised by the subtitle of this book, you now have a practical framework with which to think about the ideas flowing through your organization and how to increase their effectiveness. However, as you probably suspected from the start, leading through ideas involves more than applying a four-step method. It requires grappling with the complicated, dynamic, and conflict-ridden reality that is organizational life and culture. My hope is that the tools in this book will help you to become more adept at this high wire act of balancing the multiple ideas that define you and your organization.

APPENDICES

APPENDIX A
APPLICATION GUIDE

How to Use the Idea Leadership Tools in a Variety of Business Situations

ORGANIZATIONAL INITIATIVES
Planning an initiative
Executing an initiative
Post initiative review

PROJECT MANAGEMENT
Project alignment
Project risk analysis
Post project review

COMMUNICATIONS
Presentations
Facilitating Meetings
Difficult conversations
Enterprise Sales

ORGANIZATION DEVELOPMENT
Strategic planning
Culture change

COACHING
Coaching executives and high-potentials
Team coaching
Preparing for an interview and the "First 90 days."

APPLICATION GUIDE

This table describes how you can apply the Idea Leadership tools in a variety of business situations beyond organizational initiatives.

ORGANIZATIONAL INITIATIVES	
PLANNING AN INITIATIVE	The first three steps of **The Four-Step Method** will focus group discussions to clarify assumptions and intentions. Use it as part of the idea-vetting process to ensure everyone is pulling in the same direction from the start.
EXECUTING AN INITIATIVE	Use the **Risk Factor Analysis** tool to support formal initiative risk assessments as well as informal discussions throughout the initiative. This is especially useful for catching problems that evolve so slowly that no one would otherwise notice them.
POST INITIATIVE REVIEW	First, get a high-level sense of "what went right?" with the **Success Factor Analysis** tool. Then, apply the **Risk Factor Analysis** tool to identify early warning signs that may have been ignored. Then, document lessons learned for future initiatives.

PROJECT MANAGEMENT	
PROJECT ALIGNMENT	Create a consensus about **The Idea of the Project**. Use the **Risk Factor Analysis** tool and the **Focus and Alignment** sections of the **Four Step Method** as a framework for stakeholder interviews in advance of the project alignment meeting. During the actual project alignment event, use the same tools to generate discussions that focus on the high risk areas identified in the interviews. Also use the **Engagement tool** to clarify the divergent perspectives of various stakeholders.
PROJECT RISK ANALYSIS	Integrate the **Risk Factor Analysis** tool with other normal risk management processes to monitor **People and Communication** risks as seriously as the technical ones.
POST PROJECT REVIEW	Use both the **Success Factor Analysis** and the **Risk Factor Analysis** tools in the same manner as described for a post-initiative review (above). Be sure to document lessons learned so that similar problems can be avoided in the future.

COMMUNICATIONS

PRESENTATIONS

Your presentation will have fewer words with greater impact if you first identify **The Central Idea** you wish to deliver and then develop it using the **Four Step Method**—just as you would an idea to be delivered by an initiative, only at a small scale.

FACILITATING MEETINGS

When you act as a facilitator, your job is to guide the group through the Four Step Method as the group **Focuses, Shapes, Aligns** and **Engages** its own **Evolving Ideas**. The best way to ensure that a robust, practical set of ideas emerges from the session is to remain aware of how the four steps are interacting with each other during the meeting. Recognize this is not a linear process but that each of the steps fold back on the other as the ideas evolve within the group.

DIFFICULT CONVERSATIONS

Your one-on-one meeting to address a difficult issue will be more effective if you identify and clearly define the **Single Idea** you wish the individual to receive, with an emphasis on its **Focus** and **Structure**. At the same time, it is best to anticipate the **Competing Ideas** that exist in the individual's own mind and how to bridge that gap, particularly with respect to **Alignment** and **Engagement**.

ENTERPRISE SALES

Selling a product or service to an enterprise requires you to identify and align the **Ideas of Multiple Stakeholders**. First, you need to meet each stakeholder on his own ground to understand his **Most Important Ideas**—and to help him clarify those ideas. At the same time, to move the sale forward, you must develop a **Single Idea** that has the support of all key stakeholders. The framework of the **Four Step Method** will help you to monitor the status of this **Central Idea** as the sales opportunity develops.

ORGANIZATION DEVELOPMENT

STRATEGIC PLANNING

The first step of strategic planning is to clarify and gain consensus around **The Idea of the Future Vision** of the organization. Using the **Four Step Method** will help you to define and keep track of this idea as the strategic plan is developed.

CULTURE CHANGE

An organization's culture is simply **The Idea an Organization Holds of itself**. (see Chapter 5) First, identify the idea(s) that currently define the culture and compare it with the idea of the future culture. For a smooth transition, involve employees in this process over an extended period of time. Remember that culture change comes through evolution rather than revolution.

COACHING EXECUTIVES AND HIGH-POTENTIALS	The **Four-Step Method**, as demonstrated in Chapter 6, provides a vocabulary and framework for individuals to think through who they are, what they are trying to accomplish and how they can enlist the help of others to achieve their goals. Although the **Success Factor Analysis** and the **Risk Factor Analyses** are designed to be applied to ideas delivered by organizational initiatives, they require only minor adjustments in wording to apply to **The Idea of You-as-Leader**.
TEAM COACHING	You can increase the effectiveness of teams, particularly those who have worked together for a long time, by facilitating group discussions. The tools will help bring out issues team members have long avoided but that interfere with communications, collaboration and trust. A good place to start is to identify the **Key Ideas** held by team members and discuss their **Alignment** in terms of objectives, vocabulary, culture and structure. (It is often best to have private conversations with individual team members in advance of a group discussion, to anticipate and diffuse tensions that may arise).
FIRST 100 DAYS	**The Idea People Hold of You**, particularly if you are new to an organization, is critical to your success in an interview and getting traction during the critical first three months. First impressions are crucial during these times. It is worth the effort to think through **The Idea of You-as-Leader** (see chapter 6) and how it relates to the **Ideas in the Heads of Others**.

APPENDIX B
SUCCESS FACTOR ANALYSIS

A checklist to assess the degree to which each Success Factor is in place in support of your idea. Details on each of these Success Factors can be found in the Success Factor Analysis pages of chapters 1-4.

SUCCESS FACTOR ANALYSIS

The name of your idea:

Directions:

1) Rate how well each of the following Idea Success Factors are in place for your idea.

2) Place a checkmark (✔) next to those Success Factors requiring additional support.

3) Indicate the next steps you will take to increase the presence of those Success Factors.

Key: **1** = Absent   **2** = Inadequate   **3** = Adequate   **4** = More than adequate

FOCUS: ENSURING THAT PEOPLE ARE ABSOLUTELY CLEAR ON WHO IS EXPECTED TO TAKE WHAT ACTIONS, AND WHY.				
1.1 Communication of the process and the idea	1	2	3	4
1.2 An idea rooted in reality	1	2	3	4
1.3 An involved and committed idea champion	1	2	3	4
1.4 Strong orientation to business outcomes	1	2	3	4
1.5 Clear and bi-directional accountability	1	2	3	4

SHAPE: ENABLING PEOPLE TO PICK UP YOUR IDEA, CARRY IT WITH THEM AND SHARE IT WITH OTHERS.				
2.1 A 30-second elevator speech	1	2	3	4
2.2 Precise process and outcome metrics	1	2	3	4
2.3 Consistent vocabulary and framework	1	2	3	4
2.4 Systematic problem resolution	1	2	3	4
2.5 The idea remains in the spotlight	1	2	3	4

ALIGNMENT: IDENTIFYING OTHER IDEAS THAT WILL ENHANCE OR DIMINISH THE MOMENTUM OF YOUR IDEA.				
3.1 A well-defined Future Vision	1	2	3	4
3.2 Long range idea scanning	1	2	3	4
3.3 An organization prepared to accept delivery of the idea	1	2	3	4
3.4 Integrated alignment processes	1	2	3	4
3.5 Intellectual honesty	1	2	3	4

ENGAGEMENT: UNDERSTANDING THE LENSES PEOPLE WILL USE TO DECIDE "WHAT'S IN IT FOR ME?" (WIFM)				
4.1 Evidence-based validity	1	2	3	4
4.2 Trust-based credibility	1	2	3	4
4.3 Pride of participation	1	2	3	4
4.4 Empowerment	1	2	3	4
4.5 Commitment to the idea	1	2	3	4

Next Steps:

APPENDIX C
RISK FACTOR ANALYSIS

A checklist to assess the degree to which each Risk Factor poses a threat to the success of your idea. Details on each of these Risk Factors can be found in the Risk Factor Analysis pages of chapters 1-4.

The name of your idea:

Directions:

1) Place a checkmark (✔) next to those risk indicators that are present.

2) Circle those checkmarks that suggest a significant risk to the success of your idea.

3) Indicate the next steps you will take to mitigate the most significant risk factors.

Risk Factor Analysis: Focus

I.I-THE MESSAGE DOESN'T GET TO THE TROOPS

☐ Those who are expected to change are unaware of that expectation.

☐ Employees cannot tell you who, what or why, when you ask about the idea behind the initiative.

☐ Ask ten employees about the idea promoted by an initiative and get ten different answers.

☐ People don't ask questions about or comment on the idea during meetings, either during the initiative process or afterwards.

☐ The allocation of employee time or effort has not changed since the idea was delivered to the organization.

RISK MITIGATION: SEE SUCCESS FACTORS I.I & I.5.

I.2-THE IDEA BECOMES DISCONNECTED FROM REALITY

☐ Leaders of an initiative can't describe the practical, ground-level impacts of the idea they are promoting.

☐ No one can explain what activities are going to be eliminated to allow for the idea to be carried out.

☐ You see that nothing changes at the ground level as a result of the idea.

☐ The objectives to be achieved as a result of employees adopting the idea are too vague to be actionable.

☐ Time allocations and other resources are adequate to begin the initiative but not sustain the idea over the long term.

RISK MITIGATION: SEE SUCCESS FACTORS I.2 & I.4.

I.3-LEADERSHIP LOSES INTEREST

- ☐ Updates on the status of an initiative, or the idea it is to promote, disappear from leadership reports, and no one asks for them.

- ☐ Direct reports of leaders can't give meaningful updates on the status of either the initiative or the idea it supports.

- ☐ Resources set aside for the promotion and implementation of the idea get allocated elsewhere.

- ☐ Activities required to carry out one idea conflict with those required by another idea promoted by yet another initiative.

- ☐ Organizational priorities shift, but no one tells the organization.

RISK MITIGATION: SEE SUCCESS FACTORS I.3 & I.5.

I.4-ACTIONS BECOME MORE IMPORTANT THAN RESULTS

- ☐ Employees carry out activities required by an initiative, or to the idea it supports, but can't describe the relationship of these to business outcomes.

- ☐ Resources are expended in support of an idea, but there is no evidence of the connection between these expenditures and business outcomes.

- ☐ Documentation of the impact of the idea on the organization focuses on activities rather than results.

- ☐ Bonuses or other rewards are based on activities rather than on the results the activities are intended to achieve.

RISK MITIGATION: SEE SUCCESS FACTORS I.1, I.4 & I.5.

I.5-ACCOUNTABILITY DISAPPEARS

- ☐ There are no metrics for either progress or success in the implementation of the idea.

- ☐ Performance reviews do not reference progress of the idea or of the initiative that carries it forward.

- ☐ It is unclear to whom you can turn to obtain a definitive status report on the integration of the idea within the organization.

- ☐ Employees see no advantage in supporting the idea or participating in the initiative process.

- ☐ No one acknowledges responsibility for delays or missed objectives.

RISK MITIGATION: SEE SUCCESS FACTORS I.3 & I.5.

2.1-A SIMPLY-STATED IDEA IS MISTAKEN FOR A SIMPLE IDEA

☐ An idea doesn't move beyond slogans and posters.

☐ More resources are put into publicity than implementation.

☐ Proponents of the idea cannot describe details of implementation of the initiative or the impact of the idea on the organization.

☐ Responsibility for an initiative is handed off to subordinates with only a bare-bones description that provides little direction.

☐ People expected to take action once the idea is delivered to them can give only superficial explanations of what it is about.

RISK MITIGATION: SEE SUCCESS FACTORS 2.1 & 2.2.

2.2-FEELING GOOD IS THE PRIMARY OUTCOME.

☐ Announcements of good intentions satisfy the desire for change.

☐ General goals don't evolve to specific plans.

☐ Employees get enthused about the idea as it is rolled out, even though there is no specific plan for follow-through.

☐ Leaders congratulate themselves on a job well done after an outstanding kick-off meeting but before the idea has had any impact.

☐ Team members believe their own promotional materials with no evidence the promised benefits were achieved.

RISK MITIGATION: SEE SUCCESS FACTOR 2.2.

2.3-THE IDEA BECOMES MIRED IN COMPLEXITY

☐ The same issues are discussed repeatedly without resolution.

☐ Members of the same team provide conflicting updates.

☐ Status reports are inconsistent in format and lack details.

☐ Team members and stakeholders resist efforts to get very specific on the idea or the progress toward its acceptance and adoption by the organization.

☐ Issues are resolved through political power rather than intelligent discussion.

RISK MITIGATION: SEE SUCCESS FACTORS 2.1, 2.2, & 2.3.

2.4-MOMENTUM IS YIELDED TO ANALYSIS PARALYSIS.

☐ Initiative components proliferate with limited communication among those responsible for them.

☐ More and more data is collected and analyzed while fewer and fewer decisions are made.

☐ Interim plans are shuttled among increasing numbers of experts with decreasing forward movement.

☐ Initiative meetings process endless details with little progress forward.

☐ More thought and discussion is devoted to designing and developing the initiative than to planning for its integration into the organization.

RISK MITIGATION: SEE SUCCESS FACTORS 2.I & 2.4.

2.5-THE INITIATIVE FADES INTO THE WOODWORK

☐ Updates on the progress of an initiative disappear from executive reports.

☐ Key initiative team members gradually move to other projects.

☐ Timelines get extended and no one pays attention to them.

☐ Budgetary resources disappear or don't get renewed.

☐ The idea is no longer a topic of conversation.

RISK MITIGATION: SEE SUCCESS FACTORS 2.2., 2.3 & 2.5.

Risk Factor Analysis: Alignment

3.1-DOUBLE VISION

☐ The logical, long-term consequences of an initiative don't reflect the espoused Future Vision of the company.

☐ The underlying assumptions held by proponents of one or more initiatives are contradictory.

☐ When asked to describe the initiative, people on the same team come up with very different interpretations of what it is about.

☐ People give lip service to the official Future Vision of the initiative but act contrary to that vision.

☐ Employees dismiss a new idea as irrelevant to their work and their organization.

RISK MITIGATION: SEE SUCCESS FACTORS 3.1, 3.4 & 3.5.

3.2-SHIPS PASS IN THE NIGHT

☐ Similar ideas are developed in multiple silos with their respective proponents unaware of the efforts of the other.

☐ Employees comment that "the left hand doesn't seem to be aware of what the right hand is doing."

☐ Stakeholders, being interviewed for a new initiative, report they were interviewed for a similar one earlier in the year.

☐ A business unit addresses an issue that is probably being faced by other business units, but neglects to check in with them.

☐ Heads of business units purposely keep certain initiatives below the corporate radar to protect their independence.

RISK MITIGATION: SEE SUCCESS FACTORS 3.1, 3.2 & 3.4.

3.3-IDEAS COLLIDE SILENTLY

☐ An idea stalls but it is unclear why.

☐ Key stakeholders don't show up at critical meetings.

☐ Resources pledged to support the initiative are delayed or withdrawn.

☐ People make public commitments of support that are inconsistent with their actions.

☐ Problems are put on the back burner by those whose participation is required for their solution.

RISK MITIGATION: SEE SUCCESS FACTORS 3.1, 3.2, 3.3 & 3.4.

3.4-THE TEAM INSULATES ITSELF FROM STAKEHOLDERS

☐ Meeting formal specifications becomes more important than satisfying emerging needs of stakeholders.

☐ Initiative sponsors or other stakeholders are not invited to initiative team meetings.

☐ Team members thwart input by defensively referring to original specifications.

☐ Changing conditions and assumptions are ignored.

☐ Team discussions refer to themselves as "us" and to their stakeholders as "them."

RISK MITIGATION: SEE SUCCESS FACTORS 3.3 & 3.4.

3.5-OPEN WARFARE

☐ Discussions about priorities and resource allocations across initiatives become heated.

☐ Concerted efforts are made by factions within the organization to cancel the initiative.

☐ Executives and managers instruct their employees not to participate.

☐ Emails are used to attack or document positions rather than to resolve problems.

☐ Politics guide the realignment of an idea rather than purpose or vision.

RISK MITIGATION: SEE SUCCESS FACTORS 3.3, 3.4 & 3.5.

Risk Factor Analysis: Engagement

4.1-DOUBT CREEP

- ☐ Employees ask questions or make wry comments that suggest misgivings about the initiative.
- ☐ People make no preparations for changes in their own plans or behaviors that accepting and acting on the idea would require.
- ☐ Owners of functions or processes that would be affected by the idea take no action to accommodate those changes.
- ☐ Ground level budgets and plans for the following year do not reflect an expectation of change as a result of the initiative.
- ☐ People hold off committing to the initiative until they know for sure that it "is real."

RISK MITIGATION: SEE SUCCESS FACTORS 4.1 & 4.2.

4.2-THE IDEA IS DISOWNED

- ☐ People no longer brag to others about the initiative with which they are involved or the idea it is delivering to the organization.
- ☐ People distance themselves from the idea before or after it is delivered to the organization.
- ☐ You hear a lot of people saying, "That's not my job."
- ☐ People talk about their involvement with an initiative as an obligation rather than an opportunity.
- ☐ When asked what they have been doing, employees make no mention of the initiative, the idea it is promoting, or its impact on their own work.

RISK MITIGATION: SEE SUCCESS FACTORS 4.3 & 4.5.

4.3-LOST MOMENTUM

- ☐ Employees no longer even bother to express doubts about the initiative, simply dismissing it as not worth their attention.
- ☐ People show up late for team meetings, or miss them.
- ☐ People do not linger and talk after team meetings.
- ☐ Key personnel send substitutes to meetings.
- ☐ Team morale is on the decline.

RISK MITIGATION: SEE SUCCESS FACTORS 4.3, 4.4 & 4.5.

4.4-THE CONVERSATION GOES NEGATIVE

- ☐ Subtle, and not so subtle, sarcasm enters into conversation.
- ☐ There are more complaints raised than solutions offered.
- ☐ Lots of finger-pointing.
- ☐ Frequent gripe sessions.
- ☐ The room goes silent when the initiative's leader walks in.

RISK MITIGATION: SEE SUCCESS FACTORS 4.2 & 4.3.

4.5-VOLUNTEERS FIND OTHER CAUSES

- ☐ People do only what is necessary to meet expectations.
- ☐ The best people get themselves assigned to other projects.
- ☐ People show up late and leave early.
- ☐ People no longer ask to be on the project.
- ☐ Those who were excited to get the initiative started are not excited about implementing it.

RISK MITIGATION: SEE SUCCESS FACTORS 4.3, 4.4 & 4.5.

Next Steps:

APPENDIX D
THE FOUR-STEP METHOD

A step-by-step process for designing an idea according to the principles described in chapters 1-4 and illustrated in chapters 5 and 6.

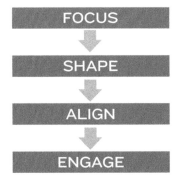

The Four-Step Method

INTRODUCTION TO THE FOUR-STEP METHOD

What is this? This is a method you or your team can use to work your way through the design and implementation of an idea. The idea may be delivered by an organization-wide initiative, by a presentation to a small group, or anything in between.

Where can I see an example of how to apply these steps? Chapters 5 and 6 apply this method to the idea of The-Organization-You-Lead and the idea of You-as-Leader, respectively. They provide detailed descriptions of each of these steps. Examples throughout the book will also give you a practical understanding of each of the four steps of the method.

How does it relate to the Success Factor and Risk Factor Analysis? The Four-Step Method applies to ideas of all types. The Success Factor and Risk Factor analyses are targeted directly at ideas carried forward by organizational initiatives. Nevertheless, you will find these Success Factor and Risk Factor analyses useful in analyzing other sorts of ideas with minor adjustments in the vocabulary.

BEFORE YOU START:
PUT YOUR STAKE IN THE GROUND

NAME YOUR IDEA, AND IDENTIFY HOW YOU PLAN TO DELIVER THE IDEA.

Directions: Use this activity to put some boundaries around your idea by clarifying in your own mind what you do and don't want it to represent.

Helpful Hint: Recognize that this is just a start. You will fine-tune your responses to these two questions as you complete each of the four steps and, as you do, you may decide to completely redefine your focus.

What do you name this idea?

What are the processes by which this idea will delivered to the organization? (Limit to a maximum of 3):

Step 1:
Focus Your Idea for Impact

Step one occurs in two parts. Be as specific as possible on each entry and resist the temptation to add additional actors and actions. You can always do that later. The purpose of this step is to force you to think in extremely practical and concrete terms of what you want to accomplish by delivering this idea to the organization and how people's behaviors will change as a result.

Step 1-A:
Identify the Purpose you wish to achieve by delivering the idea to your employees, and its short-term objectives.

Long-Term purpose: Describe why it is important for the organization to adopt this idea.

_____

_____

_____

Immediate objective: Describe what is expected as the immediate, measurable benefit if this idea is accepted and adopted by the organization.

_____

_____

_____

Step 1-B:
Define who you want to take what actions as a result of accepting delivery of your idea.

Actors and Actions: Identify three representative employees or stakeholders and indicate one specific action you will want each to take upon accepting this idea and integrating it into their work.

REPRESENTATIVE ACTOR	ACTION
PERSON #1:	
PERSON #2:	
PERSON #3:	

Notes:

Step 2:
Shape Your Idea for Understanding

Evaluate the shape of the idea, and the ease with which people can pick it up and use it as you intend.

   a. Identify three representative employees or other stakeholders who you hope will take action on your idea.

   b. For each person:
- Indicate the Shape of your idea as that individual currently sees it.
- Indicate, for that person, if the idea needs to be reshaped on the simple-complex or precise-fuzzy dimensions.

Helpful Hints: Remember that the names of the shapes and dimensions of precise-fuzzy and simple-complex are all relative terms—an idea may be fuzzy to one person and precise to another. It is more important to determine in which direction you need to nudge your idea than to decide in what quadrant it belongs.

REPRESENTATIVE EMPLOYEE OR OTHER STAKEHOLDER	SHAPE OF IDEA AS CURRENTLY PERCEIVED (Circle one)	HOW SHAPE SHOULD BE MODIFIED FOR THIS INDIVIDUAL (Circle one in each column)	
PERSON #1:	Pointed	More Precise	More Simple
	Cloudy	Keep as-is	Keep as-is
	Turbulent	More Fuzzy	More Complex
	Schematic		
PERSON #2:	Pointed	More Precise	More Simple
	Cloudy	Keep as-is	Keep as-is
	Turbulent	More Fuzzy	More Complex
	Schematic		
PERSON #3:	Pointed	Keep as-is	Keep as-is
	Cloudy	More Fuzzy	More Complex
	Turbulent		
	Schematic		

Notes:

Step 3:
Align Your Idea for Synergy

Scan the organization for aligned and non-aligned ideas that may help or hinder yours.

a. List three other ideas in the organization that may be relevant to your idea.

b. Identify the degree to which each of these three ideas is aligned to the idea you have identified at the beginning of this exercise on each of the four facets of alignment, using the following code:

- A = The idea is aligned with yours (works with your idea)
- M = The idea is misaligned with yours (works against your idea)
- Blank = neutral or uncertain

Helpful Hints: Since there are thousands of ideas floating around in your organization that may help or hinder your idea, it may seem like a difficult task to identify just three. It is best to keep the list short for now, as you can always expand it later. Ask yourself, "What idea is out there that could get in the way of mine, or confuse people?" Or, "What is a related idea that already has the support of others that I can piggy-back on?"

OTHER IDEAS IN THE ORGANIZATION THAT MAY BE RELEVANT TO YOURS	OBJECTIVES	VOCABULARY	CULTURE	STRUCTURE

Notes:

Step 4:
Position Your Idea for Engagement

Look at your idea through the lenses of others.

a. List several individuals who represent distinct employee or stakeholder groups who you need to engage with your idea.

b. Identify with an 'X' the 1-2 lenses each person is likely to consider most important when evaluating your idea.

c. Indicate WIFM ("What's in it for me?") for each person to accept and act on your idea as you would like him to.

Helpful Hints: It is better to start with only three representative employees or other stakeholders—you can always extend the list later. Try to select them, for the purpose of this exercise, so that they represent a diversity of perspectives of people who will be important to making your idea a success in the long run. For example, you might consider a high-level executive, a mid-manager and a front-line worker; or you might consider using different generational groups or people from different geographic regions.

REPRESENTATIVE EMPLOYEES OR OTHER STAKEHOLDERS	PROFESSIONAL VALUES	TEAM	ORGANIZATION	PERSONAL VALUES	FAMILY	SOCIETY
PERSON #1:						
WIFM:						
PERSON #2:						
WIFM:						
PERSON #3:						
WIFM:						

Notes:

Next Steps

Create an action plan for increasing the effectiveness of your idea.

Helpful Hints: Look over your analysis and identify some specific things you can do to increase the effectiveness of that idea. You may want to skim through some of the previous chapters for additional insights, particularly in terms of the detailed success and risk factors.

TASK	PERSON RESPONSIBLE	COMPLETION DATE

CPSIA information can be obtained at www.ICGtesting.com
Printed in the USA
BVOW10*1040141214

379253BV00001B/1/P